The
RESTAURANTS
of
NEW ORLEANS

The
RESTAURANTS
of
NEW ORLEANS

ROY F. GUSTE, JR.

WITH PHOTOGRAPHS BY GLADE BILBY II

W · W · NORTON & COMPANY · NEW YORK · LONDON

The text of this book is composed in Windsor Light, with display type set in Windsor Light
Condensed. Composition by Vance Weaver Composition, Inc. Manufacturing by R. R. Donnelley &
Sons. Book design by Antonina Krass.

First Edition

Library of Congress Cataloging in Publication Data
Main entry under title:
Guste, Roy F., Jr.
The Restaurants of New Orleans.

Includes index.
1. Cookery, American—Louisiana. 2. New
Orleans (La.)—Restaurants. I. Guste, Roy F.
TX715.R428 1982 641.59763 82-18921

ISBN 0-393-01746-X

W. W. Norton & Company, Inc., 500 Fifth Avenue, New York, N. Y. 10110
W. W. Norton & Company Ltd., 37 Great Russell Street, London WC1B 3NU

1 2 3 4 5 6 7 8 9 0

To the restaurateurs
and chefs of New Orleans

CONTENTS

CONTENTS

A NOTE ON INGREDIENTS

CONFECTIONERS' SUGAR is the same as powdered sugar. Individual chefs use different terminology.

CRAB BOIL is a mixture of mustard seed, coriander seed, cayenne, bay leaves, dill seed, allspice, and cloves, usually contained in a cheesecloth bag, which is put into boiling water when cooking seafood. It is now available in liquid form.

CRAWFISH and *crayfish* are the same. For the sake of consistency we have used *crawfish*—the most popular spelling. In all of the crawfish dishes shrimp can be used as a substitute when crawfish are out of season (between February and June).

CREOLE HOT SAUSAGE is veal sausage highly seasoned with cayenne, paprika, bay, thyme, crab boil, celery, and parsley. Any hot smoked sausage can be used as a substitute.

CREOLE MUSTARD is a coarse, brownish mustard made from crushed or ground mustard seed, vinegar, and salt. French Meaux mustard, found in gourmet shops, has a similar flavor, especially when mixed with brown mustard.

CREOLE TOMATOES are a locally grown variety that are exceptionally meaty and red and hold up well when cooked. Regular tomatoes or canned plum tomatoes can always be used in place of Creole tomatoes.

FILÉ POWDER is powdered sassafrass leaves. It acts as a thickener, a colorant, and an herb.

FRENCH SHALLOTS are local onions. Most people use the white part of green onions when French shallots are not available. I often use a mixture of one white onion and one small minced garlic clove.

HERBSAINT is New Orleans' answer to those who want the taste of absinthe without the dangers of that liquor. A good substitute is Pernod.

LOUISIANA CRAB CLAWS can be substituted by crab claws from other areas.

PEYCHAUD BITTERS were originally used with brandy as a ''cure-all'' tonic. They are now used principally in drinks and as a flavoring in cooking. Angostura bitters can be used in their place.

TASSO is charred smoked ham cured with cayenne and other seasonings. A good quality smoked ham, preferably ''Cure 81,'' will do as a substitute.

VISKO'S FISH FRY is produced and sold by Visko's restaurant. It consists of corn flour, Italian herbs, cayenne, and salt. Seasoned corn flour will do fine as a substitute.

FOREWORD

The restaurant community in New Orleans is unique compared to other cities. It is a community that works together for the benefit of all. In a city that is known for its cuisine, we know the importance of maintaining and strengthening that attitude.

This book is the work of all the restaurants included. The recipes were written by the chefs and owners and then tested in our kitchen and adjusted for quantity or clarity when necessary. The result is one of the finest collections of recipes available—not a collection of any individual but a collective contribution of many of the most talented and innovative chefs and restaurateurs of New Orleans.

My greatest thanks to them all.

—Roy F. Guste, Jr.

ACKNOWLEDGMENTS

Thanks to Mimi Carbery Guste, whose support and encouragement in the beginning and assistance in the final days were invaluable to the existence of this work.

Thanks to Sara Fuhrer, whose cheery attitude and persistence in testing recipes has helped make this project both enjoyable and worthwhile.

My very special thanks to Della Graham, without whom this book would simply not be done.

Thanks to Martha Torres, whose assistance in all phases of the photographic work has made this book truly beautiful.

Special thanks to Glade Bilby II, whose friendship, support, and true artistic abilities in photography have resulted in the visual excellence of this work.

The
RESTAURANTS
of
NEW ORLEANS

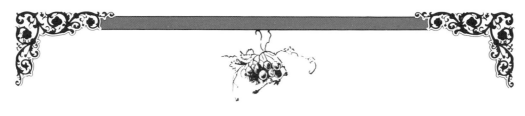

ANTOINE'S

713 St. Louis Street

Antoine's is New Orleans' oldest restaurant. In 1840, Antoine Alciatore, a young French immigrant from Marseilles, rented a building in the 600 block of St. Louis Street and opened a small "pension" or boarding house.

From there the fame of Antoine's began to spread among travelers and the citizenry of New Orleans alike. Antoine had brought his knowledge of *la cuisine Française, la cuisine Provençal*, and an ability to create and adapt the products of the area.

Five years after his arrival in New Orleans Antoine married a young Alsatian girl named Julie Freyss. Julie worked together with Antoine to build the business. Having outgrown the building on St. Louis Street, they moved to a new location, the Lacoul residence on St. Peter Street, in 1860.

By 1868 Julie and Antoine had seven children. Both family and business had outgrown their St. Peter Street residence. Antoine had for some time been planning to build his own place and had acquired a piece of land from the Miltenberger family. Antoine and Julie built themselves a building grand enough for a larger restaurant, for the family residence, and for some guest rooms for friends and discerning travelers.

In 1877, Antoine was told by his physician that he was dying of tuberculosis. He arranged his affairs and informed his wife and children that he wanted to die in Marseilles and be buried there. "I do not wish you to accompany me, for it would only prolong any sorrow you might feel, were you to watch me fail, day by day, as I neared the grave. Just think of me as though I had already died, for when we part, as I take the boat to Marseilles, we will not meet again on earth." Within three months of his arrival in Marseilles, Antoine died in his mother's home at the age of fifty-two.

Mme. Antoine carried on the operation after her husband's death. It was her son Jules, only eleven years old, who began to show the most intense interest in the restaurant. For the next six years Mme. Antoine took young Jules as an apprentice and taught him all she knew. At seventeen Jules was sent abroad to work in some of the greatest kitchens in Strasbourg, Paris, Marseilles, and London.

After four years abroad, Jules returned to New Orleans, but his mother was still not ready to give him full control of the restaurant. She wanted him to work for a while as manager of another restaurant to prove he was ready. Jules became the chef of the famous Pickwick Club in New Orleans. In 1887 his mother asked him to take over the operation of Antoine's.

Some time later, Pierre Bienvenue Roy, a wealthy planter from the country in Louisiana, came to the city to do some business. He brought with him his daughter Althea, and they occupied some guest rooms at Antoine's. Althea won the attention of Jules.

Some weeks later, Jules was off to Lafayette, to the plantation of the Roys, to meet Althea's entire family and woo her into becoming his wife. Jules was successful in his mission, and soon they were married.

It was not long before Althea gave birth to a daughter, Marie Louise, then a son, Jules, and then another son, Roy. Father Jules was a master of his art and brought the name of Antoine's to international fame. He was responsible for a major part in the growth of the restaurant. He created many dishes, the most famous being Oysters Rockefeller.

The third Jules found his passion not in cuisine, but rather in Romance languages, and became a distinguished professor of languages. It was Roy who was to carry on the house of Antoine, and he set to work learning the business under his father's careful tutelage.

In 1923, father Jules took Roy to France and to the great kitchens there so that Roy might observe and remember all that he saw and tasted. Jules gradually handed over the responsibilities of the operation to Roy, so that in 1934, when Jules died, there was an easy transition of proprietorship from father to son.

Roy continued the operation, expanding and improving through the years. He added the 1840 Room, a small, private room designed to honor the year Antoine's was founded, and the Rex Room, decorated to honor the society and past kings of the Krewe of Rex of Mardi Gras.

Roy also created and added many dishes to the menu such as Pigeonneaux Royaux Sauce Paradis.

Roy Alciatore ran the restaurant from 1934 until the middle 1960s, when his nephews Roy and William Guste, Jr., sons of his sister Marie Louise Alciatore Guste, came in to help modernize accounting procedure. These nephews are both lawyers and handled all the legal work for Antoine's. When Roy Alciatore died in 1972, Roy and Billy Guste took over the proprietorship of the business for the family.

In 1969 Roy Guste, Jr. graduated from high school, began college, and started to work part time at Antoine's. Roy Jr. was headed toward a degree in law, like his father and his grandfather, but became intrigued by Antoine's and was soon off to France to learn the language and cuisine. After a stay of a year and a half, combining study in the cooking schools of Paris and work tours in great restaurants, and becoming generally familiar with the chefs and owners of the greatest houses of France, Roy returned to New Orleans to work at Antoine's.

In December of 1975, Roy Guste, Jr., at twenty-four, was named proprietor of Antoine's. In 1980 Bernard Guste, son of William Guste, Jr., joined the staff as general manager. He had worked at Antoine's from 1967 to 1972, after which he left to gain experience in the business from other operations. Bernard worked at the Brennan's in Dallas, the Fairmont in Dallas, and the Moongate House in Mobile, Alabama, which he and his family eventually bought and transformed into Bernard's Restaurant. From there he took a position in the Food and Beverage Department at the Copley Plaza Hotel in Boston and then back to New Orleans. The family heritage remains strong at Antoine's and the future will prove the dedication of the family to this institution.

Antoine's wine cellar.

Oysters Bonne Femme

3 doz. oysters in their liquor
3 tbs. butter
3 tbs. flour
½ cup dry white wine
¾ cup chopped green onions
1 tbs. minced parsley
1 tsp. salt or to taste

½ tsp. white pepper or to taste
1 cup lump crabmeat
2 tbs. (1 oz.) grated Swiss cheese
2 tbs. (1 oz.) grated Romano cheese
2 tbs. (1 oz.) grated mozzarella cheese
⅓ cup bread crumbs

Put the oysters in a small saucepan with their liquor, and simmer for 10–12 minutes or until they are cooked, not soft. Strain the liquid from the oysters (about 1¾ cups), and set aside.

Melt the butter in a saucepan, and stir in the flour. Cook the flour and butter together for 2 minutes, stirring occasionally, until the mixture becomes foamy. Add the reserved oyster liquor, the white wine, green onions, parsley, salt, and pepper. Bring to a boil then turn down to a simmer and continue cooking for 15 minutes. Fold in the oysters and crabmeat, being careful not to break them up. Adjust the seasoning if necessary.

In a separate bowl, blend the grated cheeses and bread crumbs.

To serve, spoon the warm oyster and crabmeat mixture into either a 1-quart soufflé dish or six individual ½-cup soufflé dishes. Sprinkle the cheese and bread crumb mixture evenly over the top. Bake for 20 minutes in a preheated 400-degree oven or until the cheese is melted and begins to brown. Remove from the oven and serve.

Serves 6.

Poulet Sauce Paradis

3 2½-lb. chickens
3 tbs. butter
salt to taste
pepper to taste
Sauce Paradis:
    ¾ cup (6 oz.) chopped raw bacon
    ¼ cup flour
    ¾ cup chopped green onions

¾ cup chopped celery, strings removed
2 cups warm chicken stock or bouillon
3 tbs. red currant jelly
3 cups green seedless grapes
½ cup Madeira
⅛ tsp. salt or to taste
¼ tsp. white pepper or to taste

Rub each chicken inside and out with salt, pepper, and a tablespoon of butter.

Roast the chickens uncovered in a preheated 350-degree oven for 1 hour 20 minutes.

While the chickens are roasting, prepare the Sauce Paradis. Put the chopped bacon in a 1-quart saucepan, and cook for 1 minute to render the grease from the bacon. Remove the bacon and reserve. Stir the flour into the bacon grease. Cook the roux over low heat until medium brown, approximately 15–20 minutes, stirring occasionally to prevent burning. Add the chopped green onions and celery. Cook for 5 minutes more. Stir in the warm chicken stock, and add the reserved bacon and remaining ingredients. Simmer slowly for 40 minutes; set aside.

When the chickens are done, remove them from the oven and cut them in half using a chef's knife or kitchen shears. Remove the breast and leg bones.

Reheat the Sauce Paradis and reheat the chickens in the oven before serving.

Place half a chicken on each serving plate and top with the sauce.

Serves 6.

Hearts of Artichoke Bayard

5 quarts water
3 tbs. salt
6 artichokes
Vinaigrette Sauce:
    1/3 cup vinegar
    1 cup olive oil
    1/2 tsp. mustard powder
    1/2 tsp. salt
    1/4 tsp. white pepper
1 1/2 doz. flat anchovy fillets (a small tin
    contains 1 doz. fillets)

1 cup minced celery, strings removed
1/4 cup minced parsley
3/4 cup minced green onions
1 tsp. salt
1/2 tsp. white pepper
2 ripe tomatoes
3 cups chopped lettuce (1 large head of
    Boston or Bibb lettuce)
1 hard-boiled egg, minced
3 tsp. caviar or roe (black)

In a large pot, bring the water to a boil and add 3 tablespoons of salt. Add the artichokes, and boil for 35 minutes or until done.

Prepare the vinaigrette by combining the vinegar, olive oil, powdered mustard, salt, and 1/4 teaspoon of white pepper in a bowl and whisking together, or putting these ingredients in a bottle, capping the bottle, and shaking well.

Remove the artichokes from the water, drain, and cool. When the artichokes are cool enough to handle, cut off the stems and discard. Remove the leaves, and scrape off and retain the meat from the leaves; discard the leaves. Scrape off the hairy part of the artichoke, and discard. Chill the six hearts and the meat from the leaves.

Drain and mince a dozen of the anchovy fillets.

In a bowl combine the minced anchovies, celery, parsley, green onions, leaf scrapings, 1 teaspoon of salt, and 1/2 teaspoon of pepper. Divide the mixture into six equal portions. Use your hands to form the portions into balls, and squeeze out any excess liquid from the vegetables.

To assemble the salad, begin by slicing each of the two tomatoes into three slices vertically, and then cut the slices in half. Put one half cup of the chopped lettuce on each of six salad plates. Place an artichoke heart in the center and a ball of the mixed vegetables on each heart. Arrange two tomato slices on the plate on each side of the heart so that the inside of the slice is against the heart. The end slices should be placed skin side down.

Chill the salads.

When ready to serve, form the 6 remaining anchovies into rings and fill each with ½ teaspoon of the caviar. Spoon the vinaigrette over each salad, then sprinkle on the minced egg, and finally place a caviar-filled anchovy on the top of each ball.

Serves 6.

Clockwise from top: Pommes de Terre Soufflés, Salad Bayard, Poulet Sauce Paradis, Oysters Bonne Femme, Broccoli, Sauce Hollandaise.

Omelette Alaska Antoine

1 10-oz. pound cake
7 large egg whites, at room temperature
¼ tsp. salt

1 cup sugar (¾ cup plus ¼ cup)
1 quart good vanilla ice cream

Cut the pound cake lengthwise into ½-inch-thick slices.

Whip the room-temperature egg whites with the salt until they reach the soft-peak stage—that is, when they are foamy and can hold their shape. Gradually whip in ¾ cup sugar until the sugar is completely dissolved and the whites stand in stiff peaks when the whisk is removed. Set aside.

Line the bottom of a 12-inch oval ovenproof pan with some of the pound-cake slices. (You will have to cut some of the slices into smaller pieces to fit into the pan.) Scoop the ice cream onto the cake slices, and form into a half-rounded football shape, leaving an uncovered border of cake 1 inch around the edge of the pan. Pack the ice-cream scoops hard together since it should be solid. Cover the ice cream with the remaining cake slices and pieces. Place in the freezer to harden.

When ready to serve, remove the cake-covered ice cream from the freezer. Reserving one cup of the whipped egg whites for decoration, ice the cake with the egg whites, applying them smoothly and evenly with a spoon or spatula. Seal the edges of the pan with the egg whites.

Return to freezer while you whip the remaining cup of egg whites with the remaining ¼ cup of sugar. Make sure that it is whipped long enough to dissolve the grains. Turn the egg whites into a pastry bag that has been fitted with a small nozzle. Set aside.

Remove the Alaska from the freezer, and brown it in a preheated 500-degree oven. This will only take about 2–3 minutes. Decorate with the remaining egg white–sugar mixture. Serve immediately.

The Alaska should be brought to table and scooped onto small plates.

Serves 6–8.

Café Brulot à la Diabolique

2 lemons	2 tbs. sugar
4 cinnamon sticks	1¼ cups cognac or brandy
8 cloves	3 cups strong hot coffee

Cut the very outside yellow rind from the lemons. Remove the white part of the rind from the yellow since this will cause bitterness. Retain the rind and use the lemon in another recipe.

In a fireproof bowl combine the lemon rind, cinnamon sticks, cloves, sugar, and cognac. Heat the liquid until it is hot to the touch. Being very careful, light the liquid with a match. Stir the burning liquid with a ladle for about 30 seconds to distribute the alcohol. For a special effect, ladle the fiery liquid and pour it back into the bowl. This will create a column of fire. (See the picture below.) Add the hot coffee, and serve in demitasse cups.

Serves 6.

From left to right: Sara Fuhrer, Mimi Carbery Guste, Martha C. Torres, Della Graham.

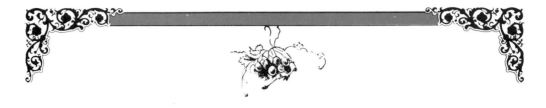

ARNAUD'S

813 Bienville Street

Leon Bertrand Arnaud Cazenave was born in the Basque village of Bosdarros, France. He came to America to study medicine, but fate had planned otherwise. He instead opened a small café on Bourbon Street. The success of the café was such that in 1918 he opened a full-scale restaurant and called it Arnaud's.

Cazenave was a creative restaurateur. He worked with his chefs to produce some of the most distinctive and renowned of New Orleans dishes, such as Shrimp Arnaud and Oysters Bienville. Being an entrepreneur with a flair for business, Arnaud earned the title of "Count," bestowed upon him by his friends and patrons.

In 1948 Arnaud Cazenave died. His daughter Germaine aided her mother in the operation of the restaurant and soon showed the Cazenave flair for the business. It was not long before Germaine was singly controlling the business. Germaine's first love was the theater, but she soon transferred this love to Arnaud's. To Germaine, Arnaud's was a stage where each day she performed two acts. The curtain opened for Act 1 and lunch began, then closed for intermission. Later the curtain reopened for the second and final act of the day, and dinner was served.

Germaine Cazenave Wells has created some of the more important dishes at Arnaud's, such as Cornish Game Hen Twelfth Night, Canapé à la Irma (after her mother), and Watercress Salad à la Germaine. In 1979, after three years of discussion, Germaine decided to hand the operation over to Archie Casbarian in the form of a long-term lease.

Casbarian, who is Armenian, was born in Egypt and schooled at L'École Hôtelière de la Société Suisse der Hôteliers in Lausanne, and at the Cornell University School of Hotel Administration. He is best known in New Orleans for his post as managing director of the Royal Sonesta Hotel and vice-president of the Sonesta Corporation.

Renovation began immediately on the signing of the lease. The first floor, which has been fully restored to its original beauty, includes four dining rooms and two bars. There is ongoing renovation of the numerous upstairs dining rooms. The new blood and revitalization of Restaurant Arnaud ensures its position as one of the truly grand restaurants of New Orleans.

Oysters Suzette

½ lb. bacon, minced
2 green peppers, seeded and minced
1 medium white onion, minced
2 celery stalks, strings removed and
  minced
¼ cup (2 oz.) minced pimiento
½ cup fish stock or oyster liquor
1 tbs. lemon juice

1 dash Angostura bitters
⅛ tsp. thyme leaves
2 tbs. butter
2 tbs. flour
3 doz. raw oysters
3 doz. washed oyster shells
3 lemons, halved

Sauté the bacon with the green peppers, onion, and celery for 5–7 minutes until the bacon fat is melted. Pour off the fat. Add the pimientos, fish stock or oyster liquor, lemon juice, Angostura bitters, and thyme. Boil for 5 minutes.

Meanwhile, prepare the roux in a separate small saucepan by cooking the butter and flour together for 5 minutes, stirring occasionally to ensure even cooking. Blend the roux with the vegetable mixture, and stir until thickened.

Place one oyster on each shell and top with 1 tablespoon of the sauce.

Bake in a preheated 400-degree oven for 15 minutes.

Serve six oysters to a plate garnished with half a lemon.

Serves 6.

Cream of Artichoke Soup

1 stick (8 tbs.) butter
6 fresh artichoke bottoms, uncooked and
  sliced
²/₃ cup finely chopped white onions
1½ stalks celery, finely chopped
1 leek, cleaned and diced (white part only)
1 clove garlic, minced

1 large baking potato, peeled and diced
1 quart water
2¼ tsp. salt
¼ tsp. white pepper
1 cup (½ pint) whipping cream
2 tbs. French brandy

Heat ³/₄ stick (6 tablespoons) of butter in a 3-quart saucepan. Sauté the artichoke bottoms, onions, celery, leek, and garlic for 7–10 minutes. Add the diced potato, the quart of water, and the salt and pepper. Cover the pot, and simmer the soup for 20 minutes or until the potatoes become very soft. Add the whipping cream, the remaining ¼ stick (2 tablespoons) of butter, and the French brandy.

Ladle the contents of the pot into a blender and liquify. You will have to do this in several batches since there is more soup than will fit into the blender jar at one time. Pour the liquified contents into a bowl until all the soup has been blended.

Pour the bowl of soup back into the pot, rewarm, and serve.

Serves 6–8.

Pompano en Croûte

Mousse:
  12 oz. scallops
  2 eggs
  ¼ cup (2 oz.) whipping cream
  1½ tbs. French brandy
  ⅛ tsp. salt
  ⅛ tsp. white pepper
Sauce:
  2 French shallots, finely chopped
  ½ cup Chablis
  8 green peppercorns, crushed
  4 cups (1 quart) whipping cream

  ¼ tsp. salt
  2 egg yolks
3 sheets thin (⅛–⅑ inch) puff pastry.
  Either make your own or buy
  Pepperidge Farm. (Roll the sheets out
  so that they measure 9 inches by 12
  inches.)
2 lbs. pompano fillets, sliced into 2-inch-
  long strips
1 egg
1 tbs. water

14

To make the mousse, combine in a blender scallops, eggs, cream, brandy, salt, and white pepper. Blend until the mixture achieves a thick consistency. Place in the refrigerator until ready to stuff into a pastry bag.

To make the sauce, reduce in a saucepan the shallots and Chablis by half by cooking 5–6 minutes on high heat. Add the crushed green peppercorns and cream. Boil for 25 minutes, stirring frequently. Remove from the heat for 15 minutes. Add the egg yolks, and stir gently for 30 seconds.

Lay one sheet of dough on a floured surface. Place the strips of pompano fillets side by side, spacing them at 2-inch intervals. Four pompano strips should fit on one sheet. Squeeze about 3 tablespoons of mousse out of the pastry bag onto each pompano fillet. Cover with another pompano slice. Cover the "pompano-mousse sandwiches" with the second sheet of dough. Cut the third sheet of puff pastry dough in half and repeat the above procedure for the two remaining fillets. With thumbs and index fingers press the dough to mold around each individual mound. (You may need to dip your fingers in flour.) The mound will be the belly of the fish. With a knife trace and cut the outline of the fish around each mound, alternating head to tail.

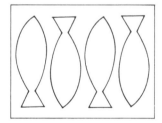

From the scraps of pastry dough, cut 6 fish "necks" each measuring ¼-inch by 2½ inches to 3 inches long. For "eyes," cut 6 ½-inch diameter circles (a funnel can be used for this). Combine the egg and the water to make an egg wash, and brush the fish with this mixture. Attach the neck and eyes, and trim the neck to the outline of each fish. Brush the egg wash over the neck and eyes. Prick semicircular indentations on the body of the fish to resemble scales. Here, again, you can use the tip of a funnel.

Bake the fish on a floured pan in a preheated 400-degree oven for 20 minutes or until the puff pastry is golden brown and flaky.

To serve, reheat the sauce slowly. Pour about ½ cup of the sauce in each plate. Place the baked fish on top of the sauce, and serve immediately.

Serves 6.

Clockwise from left: Strawberry Arnaud, Broccoli in Butter, Pompano en Croûte, Watercress Salad, Cream of Artichoke Soup, Oysters Suzette.

16

Broccoli in Butter

2 tbs. salt
enough water to cover broccoli stems
   (approximately 6 quarts)

6 stems broccoli, cleaned and trimmed
   into servable portions
1½ sticks butter

Add the salt to the water, and bring to a boil. Put the broccoli in the water, and blanch the broccoli for 3 minutes or to taste.

Melt the butter in a pan, and sauté the broccoli briefly.

Serves 6.

Watercress Salad

4 bunches watercress
6 large mushroom caps
Arnaud's Vinaigrette:
   2 tbs. wine vinegar
   ¼ tsp. salt

2 tbs. Dijon mustard
5 tbs. olive oil
5 tbs. salad oil
¼ tsp. pepper

Wash and pat dry the watercress. Remove and discard the stems.

Wash the mushroom caps and cut them into julienne strips.

To prepare the vinaigrette, combine the vinegar and salt in a bowl and allow the salt to dissolve. Add the remaining ingredients, and whisk until well blended.

Toss the watercress in a salad bowl with the vinaigrette.

Place the salad onto six chilled plates.

Sprinkle the mushroom strips evenly over the salads.

Serves 6.

Strawberry Arnaud

Wine Sauce:
- ½ cup ruby port
- ½ cup sherry
- 4 tbs. lemon juice
- ½ cup Curaçao

- 1 pint whipping cream
- ⅓ cup granulated sugar
- 1 quart vanilla ice cream
- 2 pints strawberries, washed and hulled

To make the wine sauce, pour the port, sherry, lemon juice, and Curaçao into a bowl, mix together, and chill.

Whip the whipping cream until soft peaks form. Then add the sugar, and whip together for a moment. Whipping cream always whips best when it is very cold. You may even want to chill the bowl you are using to whip it in.

Using either glass dessert bowls or large wine goblets, place a large scoop of ice cream in each. Top the ice cream with ½ cup of strawberries. (You might halve some of the strawberries if they are large.) Pour ¼ cup wine sauce over each portion, and top with the whipped cream.

Serves 6–8.

Exterior of Arnaud's with Frank Loftus, maître d', and Jan Weeks, hostess.

BEGUE'S

Royal Sonesta Hotel
300 Bourbon Street

When the Royal Sonesta appeared on Bourbon Street in 1969, the owners of the hotel wanted to bring back to the city a legend of culinary delight known as Begue's.

In 1853, Elizabeth Kettering and brother Philip arrived in New Orleans from their native Germany. Philip worked as a butcher in the French Market and soon met Louis Dutrey, also a butcher. Louis and Elizabeth fell in love and were married. They opened a small upstairs restaurant on the corner of Madison and Decatur Streets called Dutreys, which became a favorite among the butchers of the French Market.

In 1875 Louis Dutrey died; Elizabeth kept the restaurant open with the help of her bartender Hypolite Begue, whom she eventually married. The name of the restaurant was changed to Begue's. It prospered and gained international notoriety in 1884, the year of the Cotton Centennial in New Orleans.

Madame Begue died in 1906 and Monsieur Begue died in 1917, which marked the close of the restaurant.

Today the new Begue's serves traditional New Orleans fare for lunch and the most current French cuisine during the evenings, expertly prepared by chef Michel Marcais.

Pâté de Canard
Truffe aux Pistaches

1 3-lb. duck
½ lb. lean pork
½ lb. lean veal
4 oz. pork fat
duck giblets and liver
1 egg
1½ tsp. salt
1½ tsp. pepper
¼ tsp. "four spices" (mixture of thyme, bay, sage, and marjoram)
2 tbs. brandy

1 oz. shelled pistachio nuts, some chopped
⅓ oz. truffle, chopped (optional)
Currant and Horseradish Sauce:
   ¾ cup ruby port
   pinch of nutmeg
   pinch of cinnamon
   salt to taste
   pepper to taste
   1½ cups currant jelly
   1 tsp. horseradish

Debone the duck, starting from the back. Leave the skin in one piece, if possible, for use as the pâté wrapping. Leave the duck breasts whole, and cut the rest of the duck (except the giblets and liver) into ½-inch cubes.

Put the pork, veal, pork fat, and duck giblets and liver into a food processor, and grind, using a medium blade. Mix this with the egg, salt, pepper, "four spices," brandy, pistachios, truffle, and cubed duck in a bowl.

Place the duck skin in the bottom of a terrine, meat side up, allowing the skin to overlap both sides. This skin will become a covering. Place the breast meat in the bottom of the terrine on top of the duck skin. Cover with the ground-meat mixture, and, in turn, cover this with the overlapping duck skin. Place the final covering loosely since it will shrink during cooking.

Place the terrine in a suitable pan containing 1 inch of water. Cook at 350 degrees for approximately 1–1½ hours or until a meat thermometer inserted into the pâté reaches 160 degrees.

The terrine must be pressed immediately after cooking. Use a weighted top that comes with the terrine mold, or cut a ¼-inch piece of plywood to fit inside the mold. Place weights to hold the plywood in place. Allow to cool before serving.

To make the currant and horseradish sauce, mix the port, nutmeg, cinnamon, and pepper. Reduce over medium heat by one-half. Add the jelly and the horseradish.

Mix on low heat until the jelly dissolves. Remove from the heat, cool, and serve chilled.

Slice the pâté into 10–12 pieces, and serve with the currant and horseradish sauce.

Serves 10–12.

Clockwise from right: Harlequin Soufflé Sauce Sabayon, Pâté de Canard Truffe aux Pistaches, Ragoût de Crustaces, House Salad with Honey and Bleu Cheese Dressing, Crawfish Consommé en Croûte.

Crawfish Consommé

2 lbs. live crawfish
3 qts. water
3 tbs. salt
9 cups water
1 medium onion, coarsely chopped
1 leek (white part only; reserve the green
  leaves), coarsely chopped

1 medium carrot, coarsely chopped
½ tsp. thyme
2 bay leaves
salt to taste
pepper to taste

Wash and purge the crawfish in 3 quarts of water with 3 tablespoons of salt for 30 minutes. Rinse and drain the crawfish, and place them in another pot with the 9 cups of water and chopped vegetables. Bring this to a boil, and add the seasonings.

Simmer 30 minutes. Do not boil too fast or the consommé will become cloudy. (See note, below.)

When the crawfish are cool enough to handle, remove the meat from the shells and return the meat to the strained consommé just before serving. Serve plain or "en croûte."*

Note: clarification for cloudy consommé:

green leek leaves, washed and finely
  chopped

1 celery stalk, finely chopped
4 egg whites

Mix the vegetables with the egg whites.

When the consommé is cold, add the above mixture and bring to a boil. When the consommé starts to boil, lower the heat. A crust will form on the top. Let the consommé simmer until it is clear. Strain by moving the crust to the side and pouring consommé through cheesecloth without breaking the crust.

*Consommé en Croûte

Put the consommé and crawfish tails in oven-proof cups. Cover them with a puff-pastry top (puff pastry may be purchased in dough form at the supermarket). Bake at 425 degrees for about 12–15 minutes or until the dough is browned and crisp.

Serves 6–8.

Ragoût de Crustaces
(Seafood Casserole)

Begue's Velouté Sauce:
  ³/₄ lb. fish bones (from trout fillets, below)
  1 cup chopped onions
  ½ cup sliced mushrooms
  1 tbs. lemon juice
  1 tsp. salt
  8 black peppercorns
  2 sprigs parsley
  pinch of thyme leaves
  2 cups water
  1 cup white wine
  3 tbs. butter
  3 tbs. flour
½ stick butter
2 tbs. chopped French shallots or green
  onions (green and white parts)

¼ cup leeks (white part only), julienned
1 lb. fresh raw shrimp, peeled
1 lb. scallops
1 lb. trout fillets, cut into 1-inch pieces
2 tbs. brandy
½ cup heavy cream
2 doz. oysters, drained
salt to taste
pepper to taste
6 cooked artichoke bottoms
sliced tomatoes to garnish
chopped parsley to garnish

To make the velouté sauce, place the fish bones, onions, mushrooms, lemon juice, salt, peppercorns, parsley, thyme, water and wine in a soup pot, and simmer for 30 minutes. Strain through a fine sieve.

In a heavy saucepan, melt 3 tablespoons of butter. Stir in the flour, and cook over medium heat for 3 minutes or until the flour is cooked.

Stir in the strained stock gradually to avoid lumps. Simmer approximately 10 minutes or until it has thickened to the consistency of a cream sauce. Set aside.

Melt the ½ stick of butter in a large skillet. Add the shallots, leeks, and shrimp, and sauté for 5 minutes or until the vegetables are soft. Stir in the scallops and trout fillets. Pour in the brandy and flame. When the flame diminishes, stir in the velouté sauce and heavy cream. Simmer over medium heat for 5–10 minutes or until the sauce reduces to a cream-sauce consistency. Add the oysters just a few minutes before serving. Season with salt and pepper to taste.

Place the artichoke bottoms on six individual serving plates. Spoon the ragoût over the artichokes, and garnish with the tomatoes and parsley.

Serves 6.

Boston Lettuce Salad

1 large head Boston lettuce
1 large tomato, cut into 6 slices
1/2 lb. blue cheese, room temperature
1 tbs. port
3 tbs. butter, room temperature
Dressing:
    1/2 cup mayonnaise

1/2 cup yogurt
2 tbs. honey
2 tbs. wine vinegar
salt to taste
pepper to taste
6 tbs. sliced, toasted almonds

Separate the lettuce onto six plates. Place one slice of tomato on each plate.

Blend the blue cheese and the port together, then cream in the butter. Place 2 tablespoons of the blue-cheese mixture on top of each tomato slice.

To make the dressing, mix well the mayonnaise, yogurt, honey, vinegar, and salt and pepper, and serve it over the salad.

Garnish with the almonds.

Serves 6.

Harlequin Soufflé

Sabayon Sauce:
    1 egg
    6 egg yolks
    3/4 cup sugar
    1/2 cup white wine
    2 tbs. liqueur of your choice (Grand
        Marnier, Tia Maria, etc.)

2 1/2 cups milk
1 tsp. vanilla
6 tbs. butter
3/4 cup flour
1/2 cup sugar
4 egg yolks, well beaten
8 medium egg whites, room temperature
3 tbs. strawberry purée, kiwi purée, or
    Grand Marnier

Make the sabayon sauce. Place the egg and 6 yolks in the top of a double boiler. Add
3/4 cup of sugar and the white wine, and whisk constantly over medium heat until the

mixture reaches a creamy, thick consistency. Flavor the sauce with the liqueur, and cook 3–5 minutes more.

Serve warm with the soufflé.

Combine the milk and vanilla in a saucepan, and over medium heat scald the mixture.

Melt the butter in a medium saucepan, and stir in the flour. Pour a small portion of the scalded milk into the butter-flour paste and whisk to avoid lumps. Return this mixture to the pan of scalded milk, and mix thoroughly. Add $1/2$ cup of sugar, and bring it to a boil. Cook at a low boil for 5 minutes, stirring constantly. Remove from the heat and cool slightly.

Add a small portion of the milk mixture to 4 beaten egg yolks, and pour it all back into the pot of milk. Mix thoroughly, and remove from the heat.

Equally divide this mixture into two bowls. Flavor each half with a different fruit purée or one with fruit and the other with Grand Marnier, or just leave one plain and flavor the other. Cool.

Beat the egg whites in a very clean bowl until they form stiff peaks. Fold one-half of the whipped egg whites into each of the two mixtures.

Butter and sugar a soufflé dish.

Pour one of the flavored mixtures to fill one-half of the dish. This is done by tilting the dish to one side. Slowly upright the dish as you pour in the other flavored mixture. There will be a soft line of definition between the two flavored mixtures. However, to achieve more definition, a piece of cardboard may be fitted down the middle to divide your soufflé dish in half.

Bake the soufflé in a preheated 350-degree oven for 14–16 minutes. (This is a soft soufflé.) Serve immediately.

Serves 6.

Clockwise from top: Fried Catfish Tidbits and Crawfish Tails, Bread Pudding and Whiskey Sauce, Redfish Bon Ton, Crawfish Bisque.

26

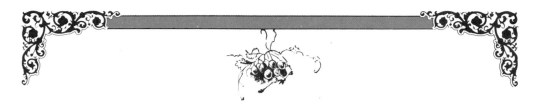

THE BON TON

401 Magazine Street

The Bon Ton was established in the early 1900s in the coffee district at 322 Magazine Street. The original owner, Albert Martin, was well known in the city as one of the great mixologists of his time, often competing in and winning contests on drink mixing. One important contest was held among three bartenders who had created important New Orleans drinks—the Sazerac Cocktail, the Ramos Gin Fizz, and Martin's own Rum Ramsey. Martin won the contest. The prize was that the ingredients of the Sazerac and Ramos Gin Fizz were revealed to him. The ingredients for Bon Ton Rum Ramsey still remain a secret, although the drink leans in the direction of a Rum Sour.

The owners after Martin were unsuccessful in the operation until Alvin Pierce bought the Bon Ton in 1953. Alvin's wife Alzina was a great cook, and Alvin himself had a winning manner and an inborn ability to welcome the clientele to the dining room.

The Pierces served breakfast and lunch until 1964, by which time the Bon Ton had gained such popularity in the area for business lunches that the owners were pressed by their customers to remain open for dinner.

In 1966 Alvin's nephew Wayne Pierce began working at the restaurant while he was studying dentistry. Wayne learned the business from his uncle. When he graduated from the University of New Orleans School of Dentistry, he assisted in the operation of the Bon Ton and practiced dentistry at the same time. In the early 1970s the Bon Ton moved to a larger location nearby, at 401 Magazine Street.

In 1979, Alvin retired from the restaurant business, and Wayne retired at the age of thirty-one from dentistry. Now Wayne and his wife Debbie own and operate the Bon Ton. Together they are continuing the traditions of one of the great restaurants in New Orleans.

Crawfish Bisque

Bisque Gravy:
- 1 cup flour
- 1 cup vegetable oil
- 2 tbs. vegetable oil
- 1 cup chopped onions
- 1/4 cup chopped green onions (white and green parts)
- 2 tsp. finely chopped garlic
- 1/4 cup chopped bell pepper
- 5 1/2 cups water
- 1 tbs. salt (or more)
- 1 tsp. black pepper
- 1 lb. crawfish tails with fat
- 1/3 cup finely chopped parsley

Stuffed Crawfish Heads:
- 2/3 cup finely chopped onions
- 1 tbs. finely chopped green onions (white and green parts)
- 1 tsp. finely chopped garlic
- 2 tbs. vegetable oil
- 11 oz. crawfish tails with fat, finely chopped
- 3 tbs. finely chopped parsley
- 1/2 tsp. salt
- 1/4 tsp. black pepper
- 1/2 cup bread crumbs
- 30 crawfish heads, cleaned for stuffing (see Note)
- 2 eggs, beaten
- vegetable oil for deep frying
- 6 hard-boiled eggs, halved lengthwise

To make the bisque gravy, make a roux by combining the flour and a cup of oil and stirrring the mixture over low heat in a heavy skillet until well mixed and golden brown (approximately 20 minutes). Stir constantly, being careful not to burn the roux.

Using 2 tablespoons of vegetable oil in a saucepan, sauté the 1 cup of onions, 1/4 cup of green onions, 2 teaspoons of garlic, and bell pepper until they are limp (approximately 2–3 minutes). Add the roux to the vegetables, and mix well. Add the water, 1 tablespoon of salt, and 1 teaspoon of black pepper, and cook for 45 minutes, stirring often.

Add the crawfish tails and fat, and simmer for 1 hour over low heat, stirring occasionally. Add the 1/3 cup of chopped parsley.

To make the stuffing, sauté 2/3 cup of onions, 1 tablespoon of green onions, and 1 teaspoon of garlic in 2 tablespoons of vegetable oil until the vegetables are limp (approximately 2–3 minutes). Add the chopped crawfish tails, and stir until well mixed. Simmer over low heat for 15 minutes. Add 3 tablespoons of chopped parsley, 1/2 teaspoon of salt, and 1/4 teaspoon of black pepper. Remove from the heat, and let cool. Add the bread crumbs, and combine well.

Stuff each cleaned crawfish head with 1 tablespoon of the stuffing.

Dip the crawfish heads in the beaten eggs, and coat thickly.

Deep-fry the crawfish heads in hot oil for 2–3 minutes or until they are golden brown, turning them with a slotted spoon.

Drain the crawfish on a paper towel, keeping them warm until ready to serve.

Taste the bisque gravy for seasoning before serving and make adjustments if necessary.

To serve, ladle the bisque gravy into a tureen or individual bowls. For each portion use 5 stuffed crawfish heads and 2 hard-boiled egg halves.

Note: You can buy professionally cleaned crawfish "heads" or body shells, or you can clean them yourself. After removing the tails, cut off the top of the head including the eyes. Scoop the shell clean, and pick out the fat (be sure to save the fat and use it in the bisque gravy). Discard any intestinal matter. Soak the cleaned heads in baking soda and water, and rinse. If heads are unavailable, the Bon Ton forms meatballs out of the stuffing, dips the balls in egg batter, and deep-fries.

Serves 6.

Exterior of the Bon Ton.

Fried Catfish Tidbits
and Crawfish Tails

Special Sauce:
    ½ cup mayonnaise
    ½ cup ketchup
    ½ tsp. minced garlic
    1 tsp. commercial horseradish
    2 tbs. white vinegar
1 egg
1 cup milk

1 cup water
½ lb. catfish fillets, cut into bite-size pieces
½ lb. crawfish tails
2 cups fish fry (corn flour)
salt to taste
pepper to taste
cooking oil for frying

To make the Special Sauce, combine the mayonnaise, ketchup, garlic, horseradish, and vinegar, and refrigerate.

Mix the egg, milk, and water.

Dip the catfish and crawfish into the egg mixture to coat lightly. Remove the fish, and dust lightly in the fish fry, which has been well seasoned with salt and pepper.

Deep-fry the fish in oil until cooked through (2–3 minutes should be sufficient).

Serve the fish with the Special Sauce.

Serves 6.

Redfish Bon Ton

6 8-oz. redfish fillets
salt to taste
black pepper to taste
paprika to taste
3 sticks butter
juice of 3 lemons

¼ cup water
¾ lb. lump crabmeat (approximately
    2 cups)
½ cup white wine
⅛ cup finely chopped parsley

Sprinkle both sides of the redfish fillets with salt, pepper, and paprika.

Melt 2 sticks of butter in a large skillet. Slightly brown the butter. Place the seasoned redfish in the skillet belly side down, and cook for 2 minutes over medium heat. Add the lemon juice. Turn the fish over, and add the water. Lightly sprinkle the fish again with paprika. Cover the fish, and cook 8–10 minutes. Remove the cover, and simmer for 2–3 minutes more until the fish is done.

Remove the fish from the skillet, and place the fillets on heated plates.

Stir the sauce remaining in the skillet. If the butter separates, add a little more water to achieve a sauce.

Place the crabmeat in another pan. Marinate it over low heat in one stick of butter and the white wine until warm.

Serve the redfish topped with crabmeat and chopped parsley. Spoon some of the butter sauce over each serving.

Serves 6.

Stuffed Eggplant

3 medium eggplants
2 medium green peppers, finely chopped
2 medium onions, finely chopped
1 tsp. minced garlic
¼ cup finely chopped celery
4 tbs. butter
½ lb. raw, peeled small shrimp

½ lb. lump crabmeat
¼ cup finely chopped parsley
1 tsp. salt
½ tsp. black pepper
⅓ cup bread crumbs plus extra for topping
2–3 tbs. butter for topping

Boil the eggplants until they are soft when tested with a fork (approximately 15–20 minutes). Halve them lengthwise.

When they are cool, cut ¼ inch from the shell and scoop out the meat. Chop the meat coarsely, and reserve it. Reserve the eggplant shells.

Fry the green peppers, onions, garlic, and celery in the butter for 4–5 minutes or until the vegetables are limp. Add the eggplant meat, and sauté the mixture for 6–7 minutes over medium heat. Add the shrimp, and simmer the mixture for 20 minutes, stirring occasionally.

Remove the mixture from the heat, and fold in the crabmeat, parsley, salt, and pepper. Cool slightly and mix in the bread crumbs. ⟶

31

Place the stuffing in the reserved eggplant shells, sprinkle with bread crumbs, and dot with butter.

Bake the stuffed eggplants in a 350-degree oven for 20 minutes.

Serves 6.

Bread Pudding and Whiskey Sauce

6 oz. stale French bread
2 cups milk
2 eggs
1 cup sugar
1 tbs. vanilla
½ cup raisins

1½ tbs. butter or margarine, melted
Whiskey Sauce:
    1 cup sugar
    1 egg
    1 stick butter, melted
    ⅓ cup whiskey

Break the bread into pieces, and soak it in the milk. Squeeze the bread with your hands until well mixed. Add 2 eggs, sugar, vanilla, and raisins, and stir well.

Pour the 1½ tablespoons of melted butter or margarine into the bottom of a heavy pan (approximately 4½ inches by 6 inches by 3 inches). Pour the bread mixture into the pan. Bake at 350 degrees for approximately 45 minutes or until the pudding is firm and a knife inserted in the middle comes out clean.

Let the pudding cool. Then cut the pudding into individual portions, and put each in a dessert dish or bowl.

To make the whiskey sauce, cream the sugar and 1 egg. Add the melted butter, and stir until the sugar is dissolved. Stir in the whiskey.

When ready to serve, pour the sauce over the pudding, and heat under the broiler.

Serves 8.

BRENNAN'S

417 Royal Street

Owen Patrick Brennan's grandfather was an Irish immigrant who arrived in New Orleans in the 1840s. After trying his hand at numerous professions, Owen took the position of manager of the Court of Two Sisters, which in the 1940s had become a popular night spot.

The success of the Court under his management encouraged Owen to begin a search for an establishment of his own. Owen found his place, the Old Absinthe House. With his own savings and financial help from friends, Owen bought the business and opened a night club. He brought in his sisters Adelaide to do accounting and bookkeeping and Ella to assist her and himself.

The Absinthe House soon became "the" place to go and was frequented by visiting celebrities and onlookers. With the success of the club came enough profits to consider new ventures. Directly across Bourbon Street from the Absinthe House was the Vieux Carré Restaurant. Owen inquired about the business and learned that its operators wanted to sell. Owen and his father leased the establishment and opened "Brennan's Vieux Carré." Soon Ella became cashier and brother John became buyer; Adelaide became chief accountant for both the Vieux Carré and the Absinthe House.

Before her eighteenth year had passed, Ella was made general manager. Brother Owen gave her a free hand in making any changes she felt necessary for improvement. Her first step was to upgrade the position of one cook, Paul Blange, to chef so that they could get on with the business of creating a cuisine distinctive to Brennan's.

The restaurant prospered, but the Brennans wanted an even more distinctive operation. The famous American writer and food authority Lucius Beebe arrived in the city on the heels of the success of Frances Parkinson Keyes's *Dinner at Antoine's*. Beebe, who was a good friend of Owen's, suggested that they could achieve great distinction and success from "Breakfast at Brennan's."

The formula was successful, and in 1955 the need for expansion brought the Brennans to their present location on Royal Street. Before the renovation was completed and the new restaurant opened, Owen died. The family, carrying the tremendous burden of their loss, decided that they would complete the work Owen had started and open on the date Owen had wanted. The rest is history. Brennan's has achieved international fame and expanded by opening restaurants in other cities and acquiring other restaurants, the best known of which is Commander's Palace.

The ever-growing family divided the businesses, and now the Royal Street Brennan's is owned and operated by Owen's sons Owen Jr., James, and Theodore.

Brennan's Oyster Soup

1 stick butter
1 cup celery, finely chopped
½ cup green onions (white and green parts), finely chopped
⅔ cup flour
1 tbs. garlic, finely chopped
2 doz. large, freshly shucked oysters (reserve the liquor)

6 cups oyster water (the oyster liquor plus sufficient water to make up 6 cups)
2 bay leaves
1 tsp. salt or to taste (depending on the saltiness of the oysters)
½ tsp. white pepper

Melt the butter over medium heat in a heavy saucepan. Sauté the celery and green onions until they are tender but not browned (approximately 2–3 minutes), stirring frequently. Gradually stir in the flour, and cook 5 minutes longer, stirring constantly over low heat. Add the remaining ingredients, and simmer for 20 minutes.

Remove the pan from the heat, and discard the bay leaves.

Serve immediately.

Serves 6.

Clockwise from top: Brennan's Oyster Soup, Veal Kottwitz, Bananas Foster, Crêpes Barbara.

Crêpes Barbara

Crêpes:
  ½ cup flour
  ¼ tsp. salt
  3 eggs
  1 cup milk
  4 tbs. melted butter plus extra for
    greasing the crêpe pan
Lemon-Butter Sauce:
  ¼ cup brown sauce (see recipe,
    page 38)
  2 tbs. lemon juice
  1 stick butter
Hollandaise Sauce:
  8 large egg yolks

4 tbs. lemon juice
6 sticks butter, melted and clarified, at
  room temperature
1 tsp. salt
¼ tsp. white pepper
Crêpe Filling:
  ¼ cup butter
  1½ lbs. lump crabmeat
  ¾ lb. peeled, boiled shrimp (cut up if
    large)
  ½ tsp. salt
  ¼ tsp. pepper
Topping:
  6 tbs. grated Parmesan cheese

For the crêpes, place the flour, ¼ teaspoon of salt, eggs, milk, and 4 tablespoons of melted butter in a blender or food processor, and mix on high speed for 1 minute. Let the batter stand at room temperature for 30 minutes or more. Spoon 3–4 tablespoons of batter into a saucer then pour all at once into a hot, lightly greased 8-inch crêpe pan. Tilt the pan so that the batter clings to and quickly covers the bottom. Cook the crêpe until it turns golden brown, turn with a spatula, and cook the other side. Slide the crêpe onto a plate. Regrease the pan, and start the process again, stacking the crêpes on top of one another. (Crêpes freeze very well and can be made in advance. Bring them to room temperature before using.)

The lemon-butter sauce is prepared by combining the brown sauce, 2 tablespoons of lemon juice, and 1 stick of butter in a small saucepan. Cook, stirring, over low heat until well blended. Reheat just before serving.

The hollandaise is prepared by heating the egg yolks and 4 tablespoons of lemon juice very slowly in the top of a double boiler. Never allow the water in the bottom of the pot to come to a boil. Add the clarified butter to the hot egg-yolk mixture, a little at a time, stirring constantly with a wire whisk. When the mixture thickens, add 1 teaspoon of salt and ¼ teaspoon of white pepper. (If the hollandaise should separate, put it in the blender or food processor, and beat it with 2 tablespoons of boiling water until it is brought back together.) Remove the sauce from the hot water and set aside until ready to use.

To make the crêpe filling, melt the ¼ cup of butter in a skillet, add the crabmeat and cooked shrimp, and sprinkle with ½ teaspoon of salt and ¼ teaspoon of pepper. Stir very carefully, and cook over low heat just until the crabmeat and shrimp are thoroughly warmed, about 4–5 minutes.

To assemble, fill the center of each crêpe with one-sixth of the crabmeat-shrimp mixture. Spoon 2 tablespoons of warm lemon-butter sauce over the filling. Roll up the crêpes, and place them on a lightly buttered baking sheet or pan. Spoon the hollandaise over the crêpes, and place the pan under the broiler for a minute or so, just long enough for the hollandaise to brown a bit. Remove from the broiler, and carefully lift the crêpes onto heated dinner plates. Spoon any extra hollandaise left in the pan around the crêpes. Sprinkle 1 tablespoon of Parmesan cheese over the top of each crêpe.

Serves 6.

Veal Kottwitz

Lemon-Butter Sauce:
    ½ cup brown sauce (see recipe, p. 38)
    ¼ cup lemon juice
    2 sticks butter
4 tbs. (½ stick) butter
6 3-oz. medallions of baby veal
3 cups artichoke bottoms (approximately

9 large artichokes boiled in salted water with juice from 2 lemons added), cut into large pieces
4 cups sliced mushrooms
1½ tsp. salt, or to taste
¾ tsp. white pepper, or to taste

Make the lemon-butter sauce by combining the brown sauce, lemon juice, and 2 sticks of butter over low heat and whisking until smooth. Set aside.

To prepare the veal, melt the 4 tablespoons of butter in a large, heavy skillet. Sauté the veal over medium heat for about 5–6 minutes or until the veal is cooked. Remove the veal from the skillet, and place it in a warm (175-degree) oven.

In the same pan, sauté the artichoke bottoms and mushrooms in the remaining butter until they are tender. Season with the salt and pepper.

Place the veal on six plates. Top the veal with the vegetables. Serve with ¼ cup of lemon-butter sauce over each portion.

Serves 6.

Brennan's Brown Sauce

1 tbs. butter   ³⁄₄ cup beef stock or bouillon
1 tbs. flour

Melt the butter in saucepan, and then stir in the flour. Stir while cooking over low heat until the mixture turns nut brown (approximately 15 minutes). Blend in half of the stock or bouillon completely, then the other half. Simmer for 5 minutes.

Yield: ½ cup.

Jackson Salad

French Dressing:
    1 egg yolk
    1½ tsp. dry mustard
    ⅓ cup wine vinegar
    1 cup salad oil
    ½ tsp. salt
    ¼ tsp. white pepper
    1 tbs. lemon juice
    ½ tsp. Worcestershire sauce
2 quarts (8 cups) packed, mixed greens (rinsed, dried, and crisped in the refrigerator)

1 cup hearts of palm, drained and cut up
1 cup artichoke bottoms, cup up (approximately 3 large artichokes cooked in salted water with the juice of one lemon added)
⅓ cup chopped hard-boiled eggs
⅓ cup fried bacon, crumbled
⅔ cup bleu cheese, crumbled
⅓ cup chives

To prepare the French dressing, put the egg yolk and dry mustard in a stainless-steel mixing bowl. Add the wine vinegar, and gradually whisk in the oil. Sprinkle in the salt and pepper, then add the lemon juice and Worcestershire sauce. Mix thoroughly, cover the bowl, and allow the dressing to stand at room temperature for about a half hour before serving.

To prepare the salad, toss the greens, hearts of palm, and artichoke bottoms in a large bowl with the dressing.

Put the salad into six individual bowls, and sprinkle each with 1 tablespoon of chopped egg, 1 tablespoon of crumbled bacon, 2 tablespoons of crumbled bleu cheese, and 1 tablespoon of chives.

Serves 6.

Bananas Foster

6 tbs. butter
1 1/2 cups brown sugar
3/4 tsp. cinnamon
1/3 cup banana liqueur

6 bananas, peeled, cut in half lengthwise, and halved crosswise
1/3 cup rum
6 scoops vanilla ice cream

Melt the butter over an alcohol burner in a flambé pan or on the stove in a large skillet. Add the sugar, cinnamon, and banana liqueur, and stir to mix. Heat for a few minutes, then place the halved bananas in the sauce and sauté until soft and slightly browned. Pour the rum on top, but do not stir into the sauce. Allow it to heat well and then tip the pan so that the flame from the burner causes the sauce to light (a match will work as well). Allow the sauce to flame until it dies out, tipping the pan with a circular motion to prolong the flaming.

Place each scoop of ice cream in a dessert dish.

To serve, first lift the bananas carefully out of the pan, and place four pieces over each portion of ice cream. Then spoon the hot sauce from the pan over the top.

Serves 6.

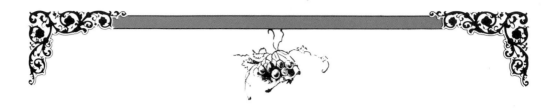

BROUSSARD'S

819 Conti Street

Broussard's was opened in 1920 by Joseph Broussard and his wife. Broussard came from the south of France and settled first in southwest Louisiana, then in New Orleans.

He began his career at Antoine's and subsequently purchased a property on Conti Street, to which he added on through the years. The restaurant became well known to locals and visitors to the city.

Joseph operated the restaurant until 1959, when he died. Broussard's continued to be operated by members of Mrs. Broussard's family until the present owners took over. These owners are Joseph Marcello, Joseph C. Marcello, Clarence Greco, and Joseph Segretto.

After closing for a while, the building was extensively remodeled, and the restaurant was reopened in 1975. The restaurant is now operated with all the tradition that Joseph Broussard spent his life creating.

Shrimp Chandeleur

Heavy Cream Sauce:
    ½ stick butter
    ½ cup flour
    1½ cups milk
    ½ cup heavy cream
    1 tsp. salt
    ⅛ tsp. white pepper
½ stick butter
¼ cup finely chopped green onions

⅔ cup sliced mushrooms
¼ cup julienned prosciutto
1½ lbs. raw, peeled, and deveined small shrimp
2 tbs. dry sherry
1 chicken bouillon cube dissolved in 1 tbs. hot water
1½ tsp. paprika

To make the cream sauce, melt ½ stick of butter, stir in the flour, and cook over medium-low heat for 1–2 minutes. Add the milk, and cook 3–4 minutes, blending thoroughly. Add the heavy cream, salt, and pepper, and cook another ½ minute. Set aside.

In a sauté pan, melt ½ stick of butter. Sauté the green onions, mushrooms, and prosciutto over medium-high heat for 5 minutes. Add the shrimp, and cook 5 minutes more over low heat. Blend in the cream sauce, sherry, bouillon, and paprika, and cook for 10 minutes.

Serve in individual casseroles.

Serves 6–8 as an appetizer.

Clockwise from top: Duck Nouvelle Orléans, Shrimp Chandeleur, Crêpes Brulatour, House Salad.

Duck Nouvelle Orléans with Dirty Rice

2 4–5-lb. ducks (reserve gizzard and
   liver from one duck and chop)
salt to taste
pepper to taste
2 medium oranges, chopped (with peel)
2 lemons, chopped (with peel)
Dirty Rice:
   2½ cups water
   ½ chicken bouillon cube
   1 box Uncle Ben's Long Grain &
      Wild Rice
   ½ cup oysters, chopped, juice reserved
   1 tbs. finely chopped onion
   1 tbs. finely chopped celery
   1 bay leaf

¼ tsp. Worcestershire sauce
¼ tsp. Tabasco
1 cup chopped carrots
2 tbs. chopped celery
1 tsp. finely chopped garlic
2 cups chopped oranges (with peel)
⅔ cup chopped lemon (with peel)
½ cup fat from the roasted ducks
½ cup flour
2 cups chicken stock
1 cup orange juice
⅓ cup Triple Sec
½ cup wine vinegar
1 cup dark brown sugar

Wash the ducks and pat them dry. Sprinkle them with salt and pepper. Stuff each duck with 1 chopped orange and 1 chopped lemon. Bake uncovered in a preheated 375-degree oven until a meat thermometer reads 180 degrees (approximately 1½–1¾ hours). Baste every ½ hour.

To prepare the dirty rice while the duck is roasting, bring the water and the chicken bouillon cube to a boil. Add the rice and seasoning packet to the water, stir, cover, reduce heat, and simmer for 25 minutes or until the water has evaporated.

In a sauté pan, combine the reserved chopped duck gizzard and liver, the chopped oysters, 3 tablespoons of oyster juice, chopped onion, chopped celery, bay leaf, Worcestershire sauce, and Tabasco. Sauté until the liquid has evaporated, approximately 15 minutes. Mix this into the cooked rice. Cover and reheat the dirty rice before serving.

When the ducks are cooked, remove the pan from the oven, and add to the hot pan juices the chopped carrots, celery, garlic, oranges, and lemon. Return the pan with the ducks to the oven, and cook 15 minutes more. Remove the pan from the oven. Place the ducks on the side, and strain the pan juices and fat from pan into a deep bowl. Skim the fat from the juices and reserve ½ cup of fat for a roux.

To make the roux, combine the reserved ½ cup of duck fat with the flour, and cook over medium heat, stirring constantly, until the roux turns a nut brown. Set aside.

In a medium-size saucepan, heat the pan juices with the chicken stock, orange juice, and Triple Sec. Bring to a boil, and add the roux.

In another pan, bring to a boil the wine vinegar and the brown sugar until the sugar dissolves. Add to the gravy mixture.

Place the ducks back in the roasting pan, pour the gravy mixture over them, and cook 15 minutes more.

Serve the ducks with the dirty rice and gravy.

Serves 6.

House Salad Dressing

⅛ cup finely chopped onion
1 cup vegetable oil
1 egg
¼ cup white vinegar

½ tsp. sugar
½ tbs. white pepper
½ tbs. salt
½ tbs. finely chopped chives

Put all the ingredients except for the chives in a blender, and blend for 5 minutes. Pour the dressing into a mixing bowl, add the chives, and stir with a wire whisk. Let the dressing stand at least 30 minutes before serving.

Serve with a tossed salad of mixed greens such as Bibb, romaine, and iceberg lettuces and watercress.

Crêpes Brulatour

1 cup milk
3 eggs
1 tsp. vanilla
½ cup flour
¼ cup vegetable oil
butter for the crêpe pan
5 oz. cream cheese, at room temperature
⅓ cup sugar
2 tsp. vanilla
3 tbs. chopped pecans

2 tsp. half-and-half
1 stick butter
1 quart strawberries, washed and hulled
  (cut large ones in half)
1 cup whipping cream
1½ tsp. vanilla
4 tbs. powdered sugar
½ cup cherry brandy
¼ cup strawberry liqueur (or rum)
6 oz. Melba sauce (available in groceries)

To prepare the crêpes, put the milk, eggs, 1 teaspoon of vanilla, flour, and vegetable oil in a blender or food processor and mix on high speed for 1 minute. Let the batter sit at room temperature for at least a half hour.

Grease the crêpe pan with butter, and heat the pan until a drop of water sizzles when dropped onto it. Pour 3–4 tablespoons of crêpe batter into the pan, and tilt the pan until the bottom is evenly covered with the batter. Cook the crêpe until it is lightly browned, turn, and cook the other side. Slide the crêpe onto a plate, regrease the pan, and prepare for the next crêpe. There will be eight in all.

To prepare the filling, blend the cream cheese and sugar together. Add 2 teaspoons of vanilla, pecans, and half-and-half. Mix thoroughly, and chill in the refrigerator for about 15–20 minutes.

Spoon 2 tablespoons of the chilled filling onto each crêpe, and then roll up.

To prepare the topping, melt 1 stick of butter in a large chafing pan or skillet. Add the strawberries; cook and stir over medium heat for 5–10 minutes.

Meanwhile, prepare the whipped cream. Beat the cream while adding the vanilla. When peaks begin to form, sprinkle the powdered sugar into the cream. Chill until ready to use.

When the strawberries are cooked, add the cherry brandy and strawberry liqueur to the pan, heat, and then ignite with a match. Lay the rolled-up crêpes in the mixture, and simmer them for several minutes until they are heated.

Place one crêpe on each dessert plate, and top with the strawberry mixture from the pan. Spoon 2 tablespoons of Melba sauce over each crêpe. Finish with a dollop or a piped rosette of whipped cream.

Serves 6–8.

Crêpes Brulatour.

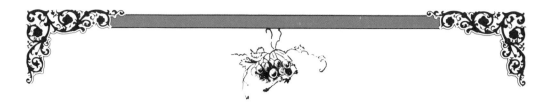

THE CARIBBEAN ROOM

Pontchartrain Hotel
2031 St. Charles Avenue

The Caribbean Room of the Pontchartrain Hotel has for many years been considered one of New Orleans' top restaurants. Opened in 1948 by Lysle Aschaffenburg, the room was created in answer to the need of his evolving business. The Pontchartrain Hotel was built in 1927 as an apartment building. But Lysle through the years converted the apartments into hotel rooms. As a hotel, he found a need for a restaurant and went about the business of creating an exquisite dining room.

The restaurant has gone through several physical transformations over the years. Now it boasts lovely wood paneling, brick walls, and pink napery.

Lysle's son Albert operates the hotel and Caribbean Room with the unceasing attention to detail that has made the operation world-renowned.

Albert's son Honoré, who is a trained hotelier, will undoubtedly carry on the tradition of the Pontchartrain for the next generation of patrons.

Louis Evans, one of the city's great Creole chefs, heads the kitchen and produces such renowned selections as Red Snapper Caribbean and Mile-High Pie.

Crabmeat Biarritz

3 cups shredded lettuce
1 large tomato, cut into 6 slices and marinated in French dressing (see Salad Deborah, page 47)
6 whole artichokes boiled in salted water

3 cups lump crabmeat, moistened with 3 tbs. mayonnaise
¾ cup mayonnaise
⅓ cup heavy cream
2 tbs. black caviar
1–2 tbs. capers

Place the lettuce on six serving plates. On top of each place a slice of tomato, and cover the tomato with an artichoke bottom. Fill each artichoke bottom with ½ cup of crabmeat. Surround each salad with artichoke leaves. Mix the mayonnaise and the cream together, and cover the salads with the mixture. Top each salad with 1 teaspoon of caviar, and sprinkle with capers. Serve very cold.

Serves 6.

Salad Deborah

1 head of romaine lettuce
2 ripe avocados, peeled and sliced
2 grapefruits, peeled and sectioned
1 can of hearts of palm
black olives for garnish
French Dressing:
    1 egg

$1/2$ cup cider vinegar
$1 1/2$ cups salad oil
$1 1/2$ tsp. sugar
$3/4$ tsp. salt
$1/2$ tsp. dry mustard
$1/4$ tsp. cayenne
$1/2$ tsp. black pepper

Line six salad plates with the lettuce leaves. Place the avocado slices and grapefruit sections in a star pattern over the lettuce. Slice one heart of palm crosswise into six pieces, and place one piece in the center of each salad. Slice the remainder of the hearts lengthwise and place on the salads. Garnish the center with black olives.

Add all the dressing ingredients to a blender or food processor, and blend or process until creamy. Serve the French dressing on the side.

Serves 6.

Dining room at the Caribbean.

Red Snapper Caribbean

2 sticks butter
1 lb. peeled raw shrimp
12 large mushroom caps
¾ cup chopped green onions
1 lb. crawfish tails
½ cup white wine
⅓ cup fresh lemon juice
1 tbs. Worcestershire sauce
4 bay leaves

1 tsp. thyme leaves
1 tsp. white pepper
1 tsp. salt
1 large egg, beaten lightly
⅔ cup milk
1 cup flour
6 6-oz. red snapper fillets
shortening for frying

To make the sauce, in a large saucepan melt the butter. Add the shrimp and the mushroom caps, and cook for 10 minutes over medium-low heat. Add the green onions, crawfish tails, wine, lemon juice, Worcestershire sauce, bay leaves, thyme, pepper, and salt, and simmer gently for 15 minutes, stirring occasionally.

As the sauce is cooking, in a shallow bowl mix the beaten egg with the milk to create an egg wash. Place the flour in a bowl or small baking pan. Dip each fillet in the egg wash and then dredge in the flour. In a large skillet, pan-fry the fillets in shortening until they are a light golden brown, turning once. Place the fillets on serving plates, and top each with approximately 1 cup of the sauce.

As an accompaniment the Caribbean Room suggests boiled potatoes with parsley.

Serves 6.

Tomato with Fresh Corn à la Créole

¼ cup finely chopped white onion
¼ cup finely chopped bell pepper
¼ cup finely chopped ham
6 tbs. (¾ stick) butter
3 ears fresh corn, kernels removed from
  the cob

2 bay leaves
¾ tsp. salt
½ tsp. white pepper
6 medium tomatoes with the meat
  scooped out (reserve the meat from
  3 of the tomatoes)

Preheat the oven to 350 degrees.

Sauté the onion, bell pepper, and ham in the butter for 15 minutes. Add the corn kernels, bay leaves, salt, and pepper. Cook 20 minutes over low heat. Add the meat from the three tomatoes, and cook 10 minutes more. Stuff the tomatoes, and bake them in the oven for 20 minutes.

Serves 6.

Crabmeat Biarritz, Trout Caribbean, Salad Deborah, Mile-High Ice Cream Pie.

Mile-High Ice Cream Pie

Crust:
  1½ cups sifted flour
  ½ tsp. salt
  ½ cup shortening
  4–5 tbs. cold water
Filling:
  1 pint vanilla ice cream
  1 pint chocolate ice cream
  1 pint peppermint ice cream

8 egg whites
½ tsp. vanilla
¼ tsp. cream of tartar
½ cup sugar
Chocolate Sauce:
  6 squares (6 oz.) German sweet chocolate
  6 squares (6 oz.) unsweetened chocolate
  1½ cups sugar
  1½ cups heavy cream

To make the crust, sift together the flour and salt. Cut the shortening into the flour-salt mixture until the pieces are the size of small peas. Sprinkle 1 tablespoon of cold water over the flour mixture, and gently toss with a fork. Repeat until the dough is moistened. Form the dough into a ball, and roll out on a lightly floured surface to ⅛-inch thickness. Fit the crust loosely into a 9-inch pie pan, pricking well. Bake 10–12 minutes at 450 degrees. Cool.

Layer the slightly softened ice cream in the pie shell. Beat the egg whites with the vanilla and cream of tartar until soft peaks form. Gradually add ½ cup of sugar, beating until the egg whites are stiff and glossy and the sugar has dissolved. Spread the meringue over the ice cream to the edges of the pastry.

Broil 30 seconds–1 minute to brown the meringue.

Freeze the pie for at least several hours.

To prepare the hot chocolate sauce, put the chocolates, 1½ cups of sugar, and ¾ cup of heavy cream in the top of a double boiler. Cook until the sauce is thick and melted. Add the balance of the cream to achieve a pouring consistency. Drizzle hot chocolate sauce over each serving.

Serves 6–8.

CHEZ HELENE

1540 North Robertson

Helene Howard married a barber who worked in the "Commercial" on Rampart Street. He recognized that Helene's style of cooking and the quality of the food that she served him were superior. They decided to open a restaurant at 1108 Perdido Street in 1942. The restaurant was moved several times before it was opened at its present location.

In 1960 Austin Leslie, a nephew, started at D. H. Holmes as a chef's assistant. The chef there guided Austin and taught him what he knew.

In 1964 Helene opened Chez Helene with her family, and Austin joined her. The restaurant met with immediate success in the neighborhood and soon was recognized by the critics as a top Creole restaurant in New Orleans. The small bar and the décor in the dining room is very homey. Helene has retired, but Austin and his small, dedicated staff continue to offer some of the best authentic Creole cuisine in the city.

Austin Leslie, owner and chef of Chez Helene, preparing chicken for frying.

Filé Gumbo

10 cups water
2 tsp. salt
shrimp heads and tails from ½ lb. shrimp
  (reserve the shrimp)
¼ lb. (1 stick) margarine
½ cup chopped celery
½ cup finely chopped onion
1 rounded tbs. finely chopped parsley
¼ cup flour

¼ lb. smoked ham, diced
¼ lb. Creole hot sausage, sliced
¼ lb. smoked sausage, sliced
3 crabs, in shells
½ lb. whole shrimp, peeled (reserve
  heads and shells for stock)
½ tsp. pepper
1 tbs. filé powder
4 cups cooked rice

In a soup pot, add the water and 1½ teaspoons of salt, bring to a boil, add the shrimp heads and tails, and boil the mixture until it is reduced to 8 cups, approximately 30 minutes. Strain and reserve. (For a richer stock, additional shrimp or crab shells may be used.)

In a heavy soup pot, melt the margarine. Add the celery, onion, and parsley, and sauté over medium heat for 5 minutes. Reduce the heat, and simmer the mixture for 15–20 minutes. Add the flour, and stir constantly for 15 minutes more. Gradually add the reserved stock to this mixture, and cook for 20 minutes over medium heat. Stir in the ham, sausages, and crabs, and simmer for 30 minutes, stirring occasionally. Bring the mixture to a boil, add the raw shrimp, ½ teaspoon of salt, pepper, and filé powder, and allow the gumbo to return to the boiling point. Reduce the heat immediately. (Filé powder becomes stringy if the boiling is prolonged.) The gumbo may be reheated gently. Adjust the seasonings.

Serve the gumbo over ½ cup cooked rice per bowl.

Serves 8.

Cornbread Muffins

¾ cup sifted flour
1¾ tsp. baking powder
½ tsp. salt
2½ tbs. sugar

½ cup yellow cornmeal
1 egg, lightly beaten
½ cup plus 2 tbs. milk
1½ tbs. melted shortening

Preheat the oven to 400 degrees.

Grease 8 muffin tins.

To the flour add the baking powder, salt, and sugar. Sift these ingredients into a mixing bowl. Stir the cornmeal into the dry ingredients, and mix well.

Combine the egg, milk, and melted shortening in a bowl, and add to the dry ingredients, stirring just enough to blend.

Fill the muffin tins ²/₃ full with batter, and bake 18–20 minutes.

Yield: 8 muffins.

Clockwise from top: Cornbread Muffins, Filé Gumbo, Fried Chicken, Stuffed Peppers, Potato Salad, Pineapple Bread Pudding with Rum Sauce.

Fried Chicken

peanut oil for frying
2 3-lb. fryers, cut up
salt to taste
pepper to taste
1 egg, lightly beaten

1 cup light cream or half-and-half
1 cup water
1 cup flour
finely chopped parsley and garlic, to
  garnish

In a large frying pan, preheat the oil to 350 degrees.

Wash the chicken in cold water, and pat dry. Sprinkle with salt and pepper.

Combine the egg, cream, and water in a bowl. Dip the pieces of chicken into the egg batter, then dredge the chicken in flour.

Add the chicken pieces to the hot oil, meatiest parts first. Do not crowd the chicken. If the oil pops, reduce the heat. Turn the chicken to brown on all sides. Cook until the meat is tender and the skin is crisp and golden brown.

Drain the chicken, place on a platter, and garnish with chopped parsley and garlic.

Serves 6.

Stuffed Peppers

3 large green peppers
½ lb. (2 sticks) margarine
1 cup finely chopped onions
¾ cup finely chopped celery
3½ tbs. finely chopped parsley (stems
  and leaves)
½ lb. ground beef
½ lb. peeled and deveined small, fresh

shrimp (purchase approximately 1 lb.
  whole shrimp)
6 oz. stale French bread, crumbled
3 eggs, lightly beaten
½ tsp. salt
½ tsp. pepper
1 tsp. garlic powder
½ cup bread crumbs

Preheat the oven to 350 degrees.

Split the peppers in half horizontally. Remove the seeds and membranes, wash, and set aside.

Melt the margarine in a large skillet. Add the onions, celery, and parsley. Sauté for 10 minutes. Add the ground beef and raw shrimp. Sauté until the meat is browned, approximately 5 minutes.

In a large bowl, dampen the French bread until it is moist. Squeeze out any excess water from the bread, and add the eggs. Mix well, and then stir in the sautéed ingredients. Blend in the salt, pepper, and garlic powder. Place the stuffing in an 8 inch by 8 inch baking pan or Pyrex dish, and bake for 40 minutes, stirring occasionally to prevent a crust from forming. When done, place the stuffing in the refrigerator until it is chilled. Skim off any fat that appears after chilling.

Fill the peppers with the chilled mixture, and top with bread crumbs. Place the peppers on a shallow baking pan filled with enough water to cover the bottom of the pan. Bake 20–25 minutes or until the pepper shells are tender and the stuffing is browned.

Serves 6.

Potato Salad

3 medium-large Idaho potatoes (1–1½ lbs.)	3 tbs. chopped fresh parsley
4 eggs in their shells	¾ cup mayonnaise
water	3 tbs. prepared yellow mustard
1½ tsp. salt	1 tbs. vegetable oil
¾ cup chopped celery	¾ tsp. salt
1 cup chopped onions	½ tsp. pepper

Peel the potatoes, and dice them into medium-sized chunks. Place them in a large saucepan with the eggs, and add water to cover. Add 1½ teaspoons of salt to the water. Bring the water to a boil. After 10 minutes, remove the eggs and allow them to cool. Continue boiling the potatoes for 10 minutes more or until they are tender. Do not overcook them. Drain the potatoes, and allow them to cool for ½ hour.

Chop the eggs. Add the celery, onions, and parsley. Mix this with the potatoes in a bowl. Add the mayonnaise, mustard, oil, ¾ teaspoon of salt, and pepper, and mix thoroughly.

Serve chilled.

Serves 6.

Pineapple Bread Pudding with Rum Sauce

1 8-oz. loaf stale French bread
water
1 stick butter, melted
½ cup raisins
3 eggs, beaten
¼ cup brown sugar
3¼ oz. evaporated milk
1¼ cups sugar
1 small (8¼ oz.) can crushed pineapple
   with juice

3 tbs. vanilla
Rum Sauce:
   1 stick butter, softened to room
      temperature
   2 tbs. flour
   4 tbs. sugar
   ⅓ cup rum

Preheat the oven to 350 degrees.

Coarsely dice the bread. Wet the bread with the water, and squeeze out any excess water. Set aside.

In a bowl combine the 1 stick of melted butter, raisins, eggs, brown sugar, evaporated milk, 1¼ cups of sugar, pineapple, and vanilla, and gently mix with the bread. Pour the mixture into a well-greased 8 inch by 12 inch pan. Bake in the oven for ½ hour. Remove from the oven, and stir the mixture down to "tighten" it. Return the mixture to the oven, and continue baking an additional ½ hour or until the top is browned and a knife inserted in the middle comes out clean.

Make the rum sauce by placing 1 stick of softened butter, the flour, 4 tablespoons of sugar, and rum in a blender, and blending the ingredients for 3 minutes at medium speed.

Cut the pudding into serving squares, and top with 2 tablespoons of rum sauce.

Serves 6–8.

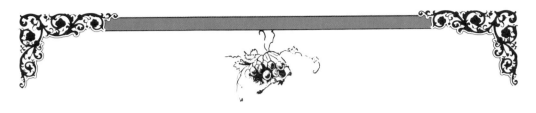

CHRISTIAN'S

3835 Iberville Street

Chris Ansel started at Galatoire's in 1966 after returning from Europe, where he worked in an engineering company for five and a half years. His father Chris had married Laurence Galatoire and had assisted in the management of Galatoire's until his death in 1964. Chris Jr. worked there until 1973, when he decided to open his own restaurant where he could create what he wanted without being bound to the older traditions of Galatoire's.

Chris first opened on Veterans Boulevard and soon felt that he wanted to be closer to the downtown area. He found an old church just off Canal Street. Chris bought the building, moved in, and opened the restaurant in 1977. The décor is still very much that of a church, with vaulted ceilings and amber stained-glass windows.

Chef Roland Huet had worked with Chris at Restaurant Galatoire since 1969. Huet then went on to assist in opening a restaurant on the West Coast. When Christian's opened, Chef Huet returned to New Orleans. Chris and Roland work constantly to conceive and devise new and interesting dishes. They have become known for French cuisine with a creative New Orleans thrust.

Clockwise from top: French Fried Eggplant, Oyster Chowder, Quenelles Sauce Américaine, Cold Redfish with Horseradish Sauce, Chocolate Mousse.

Oyster Chowder

1 bell pepper, finely chopped
1 medium onion, finely chopped
1½ ribs celery, finely chopped
¼ tsp. dried thyme leaves
1 bay leaf
5 cups oyster water (use liquor from the oysters, below, plus extra water to make 5 cups)
1 stick butter

½ cup flour
1 cup peeled and diced potatoes
½ tsp. finely chopped garlic
4½ cups chopped oysters
½ cup heavy cream
¼ tsp. white pepper
salt to taste, according to the saltiness of the oysters

Cook the bell pepper, onion, celery, thyme, and bay leaf in 2 cups of the oyster water for 15 minutes on medium-high heat. Strain, and reserve the liquid.

In a heavy saucepan, make a light roux by melting the butter, stirring in the flour, and cooking for approximately 5–8 minutes over medium heat.

In a large saucepan heat the remaining 3 cups of oyster water, and stir in the roux until blended. Then add the reserved liquid, potatoes, and garlic. Cook over medium heat until the potatoes are tender, approximately 30 minutes. Add the chopped oysters, and cook 12–15 minutes. Add the cream just before serving. Taste for seasoning.

Serves 6–8.

French Fried Eggplant

2 medium eggplants ("squat," round eggplants work well)
1 cup flour
1 tbs. salt

1½ tsp. pepper
¾ cup milk
1½ cups bread crumbs
vegetable oil for frying

Peel and cut the eggplant lengthwise into ½-inch wide strips. Dredge the strips in flour seasoned with the salt and pepper. Dip the strips into the milk, and then roll them in the bread crumbs, making sure the eggplant is completely covered with breading.

In a deep fryer or large frying pan, heat the oil to 375 degrees. Add the eggplant strips, and fry them, turning frequently, until they are golden brown. Drain, and serve immediately.

Serves 6.

Cold Redfish with Horseradish Sauce

Court Bouillon or Poaching Liquid:
  1 stalk celery, sliced
  2 medium carrots, coarsely chopped
  1 large white onion, sliced
  1 lemon, sliced
  3 sprigs parsley
  1 bay leaf
  $1/8$ tsp. thyme leaves
  1 tsp. salt
  10 peppercorns, bruised
  1 cup dry white wine
  2 quarts water
6 3-oz. redfish fillets (Redfish is a speciality

fish of the region, but any boneless fillet of fish will work for this recipe.)
Horseradish Sauce:
  1 cup sour cream
  $3/4$ cup horseradish, drained thoroughly
  $2^{1}/_{2}$ tbs. chopped pecans
  $1/2$ tsp. salt
  $1/4$ tsp. white pepper
6 cups loosely packed shredded leaf lettuce
2 tbs. finely chopped parsley

To make the court bouillon, combine the celery, carrots, onion, lemon, parsley, bay leaf, thyme, 1 teaspoon of salt, peppercorns, wine, and water in a deep saucepan, and simmer, uncovered, for 20 minutes. Strain the liquid through a fine sieve.

Place the redfish in the strained court bouillon. To poach, keep water just under a boil, and cook until the fish are flaky when tested with a fork. Remove the fillets from the liquid, cover, and cool the fish and the court bouillon.

When both redfish and court bouillon are at room temperature, put the fish back into the bouillon and chill in the refrigerator over night.

The next day, make the horseradish sauce. Blend the sour cream, horseradish, pecans, $1/2$ teaspoon of salt, and pepper.

Drain the fish and serve each fillet on 1 cup of the shredded lettuce, topped with 4 tablespoons horseradish sauce, and garnished with 1 teaspoon chopped parsley.

Serves 6.

Quenelles Sauce Américaine

Américaine Sauce:
- ¼ cup vegetable oil
- 1 lb. raw shrimp heads
- ¾ cup finely diced white onions
- ⅓ cup finely diced carrots
- ¼ cup finely diced French shallots
- 2 tsp. finely diced garlic
- 3 cups fish stock
- ½ cup tomato purée
- 1 cup white wine
- ¼ cup brandy
- ¼ tsp. salt
- ½ tsp. dried tarragon leaves (1 tsp. fresh, if available)
- 2 bay leaves
- 3 coarsely chopped sprigs parsley
- pinch of cayenne
- ¼ tsp. dried thyme leaves
- 6 tbs. flour
- 6 tbs. butter

Panada:
- 1 cup cold water
- pinch of salt
- 2 tbs. butter
- 1 cup plus 2 tbs. bread flour
- 9 oz. fresh fish, deboned, cut into large pieces
- 1 stick plus 1 tbs. cold butter
- 2 eggs (whole)
- 1 egg yolk
- dash of nutmeg
- pinch cayenne
- ¼ cup heavy cream
- pinch cayenne
- 1 tbs. brandy
- 1 lb. fresh boiled, peeled shrimp

To make the Sauce Américaine, heat the oil in a large saucepan. Add the shrimp heads, and sauté over high heat until they turn very red. Add the diced onions, carrots, shallots, and garlic, and cook the mixture over medium heat for 6–7 minutes until tender. Gradually add the fish stock, and stir well until the pan is deglazed. Add the tomato purée, wine, ¼ cup of brandy, ¼ teaspoon of salt, tarragon, bay leaves, parsley, cayenne, and thyme, and cook for 15 minutes, skimming occasionally. Strain the sauce through a fine strainer, forcing the liquid through with the back of a spoon.

Make a roux by melting 6 tablespoons of butter in a medium saucepan, adding 6 tablespoons of flour, and, stirring constantly, cooking over medium-low heat for approximately 7 minutes. Remove the roux from heat and gradually add the strained liquid to it. Bring the sauce to a boil to thicken it. When a rich consistency is achieved, remove from the heat and pat butter on top of the sauce to prevent a skin from forming.

To make the panada, heat the water, which has been seasoned with a pinch of salt, and the 2 tablespoons of butter until it reaches a rolling boil. Turn off the heat, and add the flour all at once. Stir with a wooden spoon until the dough is blended and smooth. Then turn the heat on medium, and continue stirring until the mixture becomes ball-like and frees itself from the sides of the pan. Place this dough on a plate and chill.

Purée the fish in a processor, add cold panada and cold butter, which has been cut into cubes. Blend the mixture until it is smooth. Add the eggs, egg yolks, nutmeg, and cayenne. Blend again, and chill.

Have ready a well-greased Dutch oven or deep skillet. Using one large soup spoon, scoop up a heaping spoonful of the quenelle mixture. Dip another large soup spoon in a bowl of hot water, and invert it over the filled spoon. Lightly mold the quenelle into an egg shape; do not press hard. Slide each quenelle into the greased pan, leaving enough space between quenelles for expansion. Pour against the side of the pan boiling salted water to cover the quenelles. Poach the quenelles at just below a simmer for 8–10 minutes. As the quenelles cook, they will float to the surface and turn over due to the weight of the uncooked side. To test for doneness, remove one quenelle. A knife should make a clean cut through the center. This center should be set, not doughy.

Serve immediately 2–3 quenelles per person (see Note).

Bring the sauce back to a boil, reduce the heat, and add the heavy cream, cayenne, and 1 tablespoon of brandy. Taste for salt. Add the shrimp at the last moment, and heat thoroughly before serving. Pour about ½ cup of Sauce Américaine with shrimp over each serving.

Note: If you are not serving the quenelles immediately, cook them until they are done and chill them quickly in cold water. Drain and gently brush them with melted butter so that a crust will not form. Reheat the quenelles in the simmering, salted water. When the quenelles are hot, remove, pat dry with a towel, and serve.

Serves 6.

Dining Room at Christian's.

Chocolate Mousse

9 oz. vanilla sweet chocolate (commercially available chocolate flavored with vanilla)
3 tbs. water

3 egg whites
¾ cup sugar
1½ cups whipping cream

Melt the chocolate with the water in the top of a double boiler. Set the melted chocolate aside to cool to room temperature.

Place the egg whites and sugar in a mixing bowl that has been put over a pan of hot water (double-boiler style). Stir constantly until the sugar is dissolved. Remove the mixing bowl from the pan of hot water. Beat the mixture at high speed until it stands in stiff peaks when the beaters are lifted from bowl. (The meringue will be creamy and glossy-looking.) Carefully fold the cooled chocolate into the meringue with a rubber spatula. When blended, place mixture in the refrigerator, and chill it for 20 minutes.

While the chocolate-meringue mixture is chilling, place the cream in the freezer, and allow it to chill for 15 minutes. Then, whip the cream at high speed until it forms peaks. Fold the whipped cream into the chocolate-meringue mixture until it is blended. Spoon the mousse into individual dessert dishes, and serve well chilled.

Serves 6.

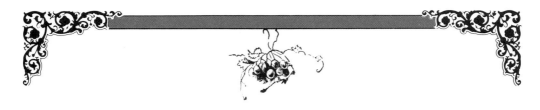

COMMANDER'S PALACE

1403 Washington Avenue

In the heart of the Garden District stands the magnificent Commander's Palace. Opened in 1880 by Emile Commander, the business occupies a beautiful Victorian mansion, now painted a brilliant shade of turquoise (if you haven't noticed).

The ownership passed from Commander to the Giarrantano family. In 1944 it was purchased by Elinor and Frank Moran, who expanded and enlarged the operation through the years. The second floor was transformed from living quarters into dining rooms, and the neighboring lot became a large patio.

After the death of Frank Moran, Commander's was sold to Ella, Adelaide, John, and Dick Brennan. In 1974 the Brennans totally renovated the heavy Victorian interior and turned it into a bright, colorful one.

The institution of "jazz brunch" was created here by the Brennans, who continue their flair for ingenuity and their striving for excellence.

Garlic Bread

1 loaf French bread, about 14 inches long
½ cup butter

1 tsp. garlic powder
¼ cup parsley, finely chopped
¼ cup freshly grated Parmesan cheese

Slice the French bread lengthwise.

Melt the butter in a small skillet, add the garlic powder, and heat for 2 minutes. Brush the butter-garlic mixture on the cut side of the French bread halves. Sprinkle the bread with parsley and Parmesan cheese. Cut each half crosswise into 1-inch slices. Heat the bread in a 375-degree oven for 5–8 minutes.

Serve immediately.

Serves 6.

Oysters Marinière

36 oysters, reserve ½ cup of the liquor
1 cup white wine or Chablis
1 cup minced French shallots
½ cup minced parsley
½ tsp. black pepper

salt to taste (you may not need any if you
   use salty oysters)
1 stick softened butter creamed with
   ⅓ cup flour

In a shallow pan, poach the oysters in the reserved oyster liquor to which has been added the wine, shallots, parsley, pepper, and salt. Bring the mixture to a boil, and cook 1 minute. Add the butter-flour mixture, and stir gently until thoroughly blended. Continue cooking until the floury taste is gone.

Serve as an appetizer or entrée with French bread.

Serves 6.

Black Forest Escargot Soup

4 tbs. butter
¼ cup minced French shallots
1½ tbs. minced garlic
½ lb. mushrooms, cleaned and finely
   chopped
1 cup white wine
1 cup beef broth
1 cup chicken broth
1 cup whipping cream

3½ oz. minced escargots
1 tbs. minced green onion
3 tbs. minced parsley
½ tsp. salt or to taste
¼ tsp. white pepper or to taste
4 tbs. softened butter creamed with
   3 tbs. flour
2 tsp. Pernod
3½ oz. whole escargots

In a heavy saucepan heat the butter over a low flame. Add the shallots, garlic, and mushrooms. Sauté for 2 minutes or until tender. Pour in the wine and the broths, and simmer for 15 minutes.

Add the cream, chopped escargots, green onion, parsley, salt, and pepper. Blend in the butter-flour mixture. Add the Pernod. Let the soup simmer over low heat 1–2 minutes. Do not boil. Add the whole escargots, and serve.

Serves 6.

Clockwise from top: White Chocolate Mousse with Raspberry Sauce, Oysters Marinière, Garlic Bread, Trout in Leek Sauce, Commander's Salad, Black Forest Escargot Soup.

Trout in Leek Sauce

3 sticks (12 oz.) butter
18 2-oz. trout fillets
1½ cups leeks (white part only), julienned
1½ cups white onions, julienned
¾ cup tomato, peeled, seeded, and cut
 into thin strips
¼ tsp. orégano
¼ tsp. salt
½ tsp. garlic powder
½ tsp. black pepper

⅔ tsp. cayenne pepper
¼ tsp. powdered thyme
⅛ tsp. paprika
½ tsp. onion powder
1½ cups white wine
1½ cups greatly reduced fish stock
18 fresh whole mushrooms, stems
 removed
1½ cups heavy cream

Place all the ingredients except the cream in a large pan. Simmer, covered, for 5–6 minutes or until the fish is done, being careful not to overcook the fish. Remove the fish from the pan to six warm plates, placing three fillets on each plate. Place one mushroom on each fillet.

Cook and stir the leek sauce, uncovered, over relatively high heat until the liquid is reduced. Add the cream, and simmer the sauce until it is reduced again and a thick-cream-sauce consistency is achieved. Top each serving of fish and mushrooms with ½ cup of sauce, and serve.

Serves 6.

White Chocolate Mousse
with Raspberry Sauce

Raspberry Sauce:
  1 cup fresh raspberries
  ¼ cup sugar
  ¼ cup brandy
White Chocolate Mousse:
  6 oz. white chocolate (appropriate for melting)
  1½ cups heavy cream, ice cold

¼ cup confectioners' sugar
8 egg whites, room temperature
½ tsp. cream of tartar
¼ cup granulated sugar
2 tbs. heavy cream
shaved semisweet dark chocolate, for garnish

Make the raspberry sauce first. In a saucepan combine the raspberries and sugar. Bring to a boil, reduce to a simmer, and cook for 2 minutes. Flame with the brandy. Stir until the flame is extinguished.

To prepare the mousse, slowly melt the chocolate in a double boiler over very low heat. When melted, remove the chocolate from the heat.

Whip 1½ cups of cream until soft peaks form. Then add the confectioners' sugar, and whip until stiff peaks form.

Whip the egg whites in a bowl with the cream of tartar, gradually adding the granulated sugar until stiff peaks form. Do not overbeat.

Cool the melted chocolate slightly. Add the 2 tablespoons of heavy cream to the chocolate to achieve a pouring consistency. Slowly add the chocolate to the whipped cream; fold in gently. Fold the egg whites and chocolate-cream mixture together gently.

To serve, spoon 2 tablespoons of raspberry sauce into the bottoms of six 1-cup wine glasses. Spoon the mousse over this sauce.

Chill several hours before serving.

Garnish with shaved semisweet dark chocolate.

Serves 6.

CORINNE DUNBAR'S

1617 St. Charles Avenue

After the death of her husband, finances became such that Corinne Dunbar, who had been known as an excellent hostess, opened her home to diners. With her faithful cook of many years and her treasured family recipes, she began what is a truly unique restaurant. The lovely Victorian home on St. Charles Avenue which today houses the restaurant has been maintained to serve a haute Créole repast just as it was done by Corinne Dunbar.

After Mrs. Dunbar's death, her daughter Katherine ran the restaurant until handing it over to her cousin, Jim Plauche, who is now the proprietor.

From being greeted by the butler at the door, to being served apéritifs in the parlor, to feasting on the set dinner in the lovely dining room, one always feels like an invited guest in a friend's home. A very noncommercial restaurant, Corinne Dunbar's stands proudly today as a reminder of times past.

Dining room with coffee and petits fours.

Oysters Carnaval

5 cups minced onions
½ tbs. minced garlic
1 bay leaf, minced
4 stalks celery, minced
⅛ tsp. thyme leaves
10 tbs. butter
4 doz. oysters, strained (reserve the liquor) and chopped

1½ cups bread crumbs
36 oyster half shells, boiled and scrubbed
18 strips bacon, precooked until crispy but not too brown; drained, with each strip cut in half
6 lemon wedges, for garnish

In an iron skillet sauté the minced onion, garlic, bay leaf, celery, and thyme in 6 tablespoons butter for about 15 minutes. Add the chopped oysters. Moisten 1 cup of bread crumbs with approximately 1 cup of the oyster liquor. Add to the above. Simmer for 20–30 minutes. Add 4 tablespoons butter, and cook until the butter is melted.

Fill the oyster shells with the mixture, and sprinkle the remaining ½ cup of bread crumbs over the top. Top with the bacon pieces.

To serve, heat the oysters in a 375-degree oven for 10–15 minutes or until they are hot. Serve 6 oysters per portion. Garnish each platter with a lemon wedge.

Serves 6.

Red Bean Soup

½ cup chopped onion
2 tbs. butter
½ lb. dried red kidney beans
1 gallon (16 cups) water
2 cloves of garlic, finely chopped
⅔ cup chopped celery
2 bay leaves
¼ tsp. thyme leaves

1 tsp. Worcestershire sauce
½ lb. ham, ground fine
2 tsp. salt or to taste
¾ tsp. black pepper
6 tbs. claret
6 lemon slices, for garnish
1 sieved hard-boiled egg, for garnish

In a soup pot, sauté the onion in butter for 2–3 minutes or until slightly browned. Add the kidney beans, water, garlic, celery, bay leaves, thyme, and Worcestershire sauce, and simmer for 3 hours or until the beans are cooked. Remove the bay leaves, and force the mixture through a sieve. Place the mixture back in the pot, and add the ham, salt, and pepper. (At this point, you may decide to thin out soup with more water. Readjust the salt and pepper if you do.) Heat thoroughly.

Place 1 tablespoon claret in the bottom of each of six cups or bowls. Pour the soup into the cups or bowls, and garnish each portion with a lemon slice and sieved egg.

Serves 6.

Chicken Breast Maitland

salt to taste
pepper to taste
8 whole chicken breasts
2 cups chicken stock
¼ lb. pork sausage, block or patty

⅓ cup chopped white onion
1 tbs. Kitchen Bouquet
1 tbs. flour blended with ½ tbs. water
¼ lb. pecans, chopped
2 tbs. sherry

Rub salt and pepper on the chicken breasts. Place the breasts in a baking pan. Bake the chicken and 1 cup of chicken stock uncovered, in a preheated 350-degree oven for 15 minutes. Cover the baking pan, and steam the chicken 15–20 minutes until done. The chicken will not be browned.

Brown the sausage in a frying pan, remove and reserve it.

Brown the onions in the sausage grease. You may need to add some butter to prevent sticking.

Blend 1 cup of chicken stock in a blender with the onions and sausage. Pour the mixture back into the frying pan, and bring it to a boil. Stir in the Kitchen Bouquet and the flour blended with the water. Add the chopped pecans to the mixture.

Add the sherry to the sauce just before serving it over the warmed chicken breasts. (If the sauce is too thick, thin it out with ½ cup of chicken stock.)

Serves 8.

Banana Puffs, Oysters Dunbar, Chicken Breast Maitland, Red Bean Soup,
Biscuits. Birds of Paradise in background.

Gumbo Gouter

1 tbs. shortening or 1 1/2 oz. salt pork,
  coarsely chopped plus 1 tsp. shortening
1 large eggplant, peeled, coarsely chopped
3 green peppers, seeded, coarsely chopped
1/2 lb. okra, coarsely chopped
2 large onions, coarsely chopped
1 14-oz. can whole tomatoes plus juice
1 clove garlic, minced

1/2 tsp. sugar
2 tsp. salt
3/4 tsp. black pepper
optional: 1/2 lb. cooked shrimp (makes a
  heartier course—1 lb. uncooked shrimp
  with shells and heads yields 1/2 lb.
  cooked, peeled shrimp)

In a large saucepan, melt the shortening and/or render the fat from the salt pork.
Add the remaining ingredients except the shrimp. Cover the gumbo tightly, and simmer it for 1 1/2 hours, stirring often to avoid burning. During the last 10 minutes, cook
the gumbo uncovered to reduce the liquid. Gumbo Gouter should have a casserole
consistency. Just before serving add the cooked shrimp.

Serves 6.

70

Biscuits

2 cups flour
1 tbs. baking powder
3 tbs. sugar
2 tsp. salt

5 tbs. shortening
¾ cup milk
2 tbs. butter, melted

Mix all the dry ingredients together. Cut in the shortening. Add the milk, and mix until a ball of dough is formed. Sprinkle in enough flour to get the dough out of the bowl. On a floured board roll the dough out to ¼ inch thickness. Cut out the biscuits with a 2¼-inch circular cutter or a glass. Lay the biscuits on a greased cookie sheet. Brush the tops of the biscuits with melted butter. Bake the biscuits in a preheated 450-degree oven for 10–15 minutes or until they are lightly browned. These biscuits are intentionally thin.

Yield: 25–28 biscuits.

Sherried Bananas

6 firm bananas
6 tbs. butter for frying
1 cup sugar
2 cups boiling water

2 tbs. cornstarch
3 cloves
½ lemon, sliced
2 tbs. sherry

Peel and cut the bananas in half lengthwise and then in half again crosswise. Melt the butter in a skillet, and fry the bananas until they are golden brown. Remove the bananas from the pan. Add ½ cup of the sugar to the remaining butter in the pan, and stir constantly over moderate heat until the sugar melts. Add the other ½ cup sugar, and stir as before until it melts. Add the boiling water very slowly to the sugar-butter mixture so that the mixture does not boil over. Simmer 10 minutes. Remove a small amount of the sugar water from the pan, and dissolve the cornstarch in it. Return the cornstarch mixture to the pan, and simmer 2–3 minutes. Add the cloves, lemon slices, and sherry. Simmer 2–3 minutes more.

Add the bananas to the pan to heat. Serve.

Serves 6.

COURT OF TWO SISTERS

613 Royal Street

Two widowed sisters, Bertha and Emma Camors, made their home at 613 Royal Street and in 1886 opened a shop on the ground floor called the Shop of the Two Sisters. They sold carnival costumes, formal gowns, lace, novelties, and imports from Paris. They also served tea and cakes to favorite customers in the courtyard.

The sisters have been described as fine ladies who dressed beautifully and were the epitome of cultured, aristocratic Creoles. They died within two months of each other in 1924.

The property was inherited by the Delvalle family and in 1925 was purchased by New Orleans writer Natalie Scott. Since then the property has passed through five ownerships, during which time it was developed into a restaurant.

In 1963 Joe Fein, Jr. acquired the property and immediately set about instituting new concepts which enabled the Court of Two Sisters to progress to its current reputation in the New Orleans restaurant community. Today the second generation of Feins, sons Joe and Jerry, continue the traditions set by their father.

Statue of the Court of Two Sisters.

Escargots aux Champignons

1½ sticks butter, softened
1 tsp. minced green onions
1 tsp. (2 cloves) minced garlic
1 tsp. minced parsley
½ tsp. salt

¼ tsp. pepper
1 tbs. heavy cream
1 tbs. vermouth
24 fresh mushroom caps
24 snails, washed

Cream the softened butter with the green onions, garlic, parsley, salt, pepper, cream, and vermouth.

Remove the stems from the mushrooms. Stuff each mushroom cap with an escargot. Cover with a spoonful of the butter mixture. Broil for 6–8 minutes.

Serves 6.

Shrimp Toulouse

1 stick (¼ lb.) butter, clarified
½ cup chopped green onions
½ cup diced green pepper
¼ cup diced pimiento
¼ cup finely chopped celery
1 cup sliced mushrooms
3 lbs. peeled and deveined raw shrimp

1 cup white wine
1 tsp. salt
½ tsp. white pepper
¼ cup chopped parsley
¼ tsp. dill weed
3 cups cooked rice

Heat the clarified butter in a pan. Add the green onions, green pepper, pimiento, celery, mushrooms, and shrimp. Simmer the mixture for 10 minutes. Add the wine, salt, and pepper, and simmer the mixture an additional 5 minutes. Add the parsley and dill.

Serve over warm rice.

Serves 6.

Avocado Romanoff

3 ripe avocados
6 lettuce leaves
²/₃ cup sour cream

1½–2 oz. caviar (black)
6 pimiento strips, drained

Split the avocados, remove the pits, and peel. Lay each avocado half on a lettuce leaf, and fill each cavity with sour cream. Circle the sour cream in each avocado with a line of caviar. Lay a pimiento strip over the sour cream.

Serves 6.

Clockwise from top: Shrimp Toulouse, Escargots aux Champignons, Avocado Romanoff, Crêpes Rivas.

Crêpes Rivas

Crêpes:
- 2 large eggs
- 1 cup milk
- ½ cup flour
- 1 tbs. sugar
- ⅛ tsp. salt
- 2 tbs. melted butter
- 1 tbs. cognac or brandy
- butter for the crêpe pan

Filling and Topping:
- 1 stick plus 2 tbs. (10 tbs.) butter
- 1 cup brown sugar
- ⅓ cup banana liqueur
- 6 small bananas
- ¾ cup coarsely chopped pecans
- ⅓ cup brandy

Beat the eggs and milk until they are blended. Combine the flour, sugar, and salt, and gradually beat the liquid into them, making a smooth batter. Add the melted butter and cognac or brandy. The batter should have the consistency of heavy cream. Let the mixture stand ½ hour.

Brush a hot 6-inch crêpe pan with some butter. Pour 2 tablespoons of premeasured batter into the pan, and quickly tip the pan to coat the bottom evenly with the batter. When the crêpe is lightly browned on the bottom, turn it and brown the other side. (See Note.)

In a large frying pan melt 10 tablespoons of butter, and blend in the brown sugar. Stir the mixture over low heat until the sugar is dissolved. Add banana liqueur.

Slice the bananas in half lengthwise. Roll each half in a crêpe. Place all 12 crêpes in the sauce, and sprinkle them with pecans. Simmer the crêpes gently for 8 minutes, turning once. Pour the brandy into the pan, and flame. Remove the crêpes from the heat, and serve immediately.

Note: If using an 8-inch crêpe pan, use a larger amount (3–4 tablespoons) of batter for each crêpe. The bananas will not need to be sliced. Serve one crêpe per person.

Serves 6.

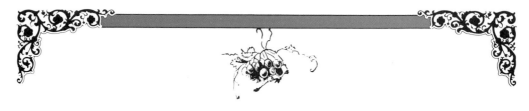

DOOKY CHASE

2301 Orleans Avenue

In 1941, Dooky Chase and his wife Emily procured a five-hundred-dollar loan from the Regal Brewery and with that sum opened a sandwich shop and bar. They became one of the first New Orleans restaurants to cater to the black community. At first, it was difficult for the Chases to get the local blacks to come to the restaurant, since this community preferred to dine at home. Most of the delicious hot sausage or fried oyster sandwiches were served on a take-out basis in the beginning.

However, the Chase family was well respected in the neighborhood, and soon the tiny place was very crowded. The clientele felt at home in their friends' restaurant. Customers began requesting meals such as fried chicken or oysters. The Chases obliged and in 1946 opened a more formal dining area in the building.

Dooky Chase II, while pursuing a career in music, often helped his parents in the restaurant. His wife Leah had begun to develop a great interest in this restaurant, having worked at others in the area. In the 1950s Leah Chase began assisting her in-laws at Dooky Chase.

Relying on her good judgment of food and her strong sense of taste, Leah worked steadily to improve and expand Dooky Chase and build it into a fine establishment.

Because of its innovative beginnings and through the efforts of its second generation, today Dooky Chase is a restaurant that is respected by and that caters to the entire New Orleans community. Leah and Dooky's daughter Emily is assisting in the restaurant and continuing, for a third generation, to offer the warmth and hospitality that have made Dooky Chase what it is today.

Vegetable Salad Bowl

1 envelope unflavored gelatin
¼ cup cold water
½ cup boiling water
¾ cup mayonnaise
¼ cup Wishbone Italian Salad Dressing
⅛ tsp. dill weed

½ cup diced boiled potatoes
¼ cup diced, cooked carrots
¼ cup cooked green peas
¼ cup diced red apple, unpeeled
lettuce
tomato wedges, for garnish

Mix the gelatin and cold water in a medium-sized bowl. Let the mixture stand for 1 minute. Add the boiling water, and stir until the gelatin is completely dissolved. Pour the mixture into a mixing bowl, and add the mayonnaise, Italian dressing, and dill weed. Mix well. Add the potatoes, carrots, peas, and apple, and continue to mix. Pour into six individual molds, and chill. Unmold the salads, and serve them on beds of lettuce, garnished with tomato wedges.

Serves 6.

Mrs. Leah Chase (center), chef and owner of Dooky Chase.

French-Style Green Beans

4 tbs. butter	2 cups water
½ lb. diced smoked ham	2 lbs. French-cut string beans
½ large onion, finely chopped	1 tsp. salt
6 small new potatoes	¼ tsp. cayenne

Melt the butter in a saucepan. Add the ham, and cook for 5 minutes. Add the onion, and sauté until it becomes translucent. Add the potatoes and water. Cover and cook for approximately 10 minutes or until the potatoes are tender. Add the string beans, salt, and cayenne, and cook 20 minutes more over medium heat.

Serves 6.

Roulades of Veal
with Oyster Dressing

3 doz. oysters and their liquor	1 tsp. paprika
water	1½ tsp. salt
3 cups cubed stale bread	½ tsp. cayenne
1 cup chopped onions	¼ cup vegetable oil
½ cup chopped celery	2 veal rounds (each ½ inch thick)
½ tsp. ground thyme	salt to taste
2 cloves garlic, minced	pepper to taste
3 tbs. chopped parsley	

Drain the oysters, saving the liquor. Put the oyster liquor in a measuring cup, and add enough water to equal 1½ cups. Pour this over the bread, and let the bread soak until it becomes soft.

Chop the oysters, and add them to the bread along with the onions, celery, thyme, garlic, parsley, paprika, salt and cayenne. Mix well.

Heat the oil in a pot, and add the oyster mixture. Cook the mixture until the onions become translucent. Remove the pot from the heat, and let the dressing cool.

Clockwise from top right: Strawberry and Chocolate Ice Box Cake, Roulades of Veal, House Salad, French-Style String Beans.

Cut each round of veal into 3 slices. Pound these a little, and lightly sprinkle them with salt and pepper. Divide the oyster dressing among the pieces of veal. Roll the veal around the dressing, and secure each roll with a toothpick. Place the roulades of veal in a greased pan, and cover. Bake the veal at 350 degrees for 35 minutes. Remove the cover, and cook 10 minutes longer, basting with the pan juices.

Serves 6.

Strawberry and Chocolate Ice Box Cake

4 egg whites
½ tsp. cream of tartar
1⅓ cups sugar
6 oz. semisweet chocolate

3 tbs. water
3 cups whipping cream
1 pint fresh strawberries, sliced

Preheat the oven to 250 degrees.

To make three meringue patterns, line a baking sheet with waxed paper, and trace three circles using an 8-inch cake pan as your guide. Set the sheet aside until the meringue is ready.

To make the meringue, beat the egg whites until they are foamy. Add the cream of tartar, and beat the egg whites until they reach the soft-peak stage. Slowly add 1 cup of sugar to the egg whites, continuing to beat until the meringue is stiff.

With the meringue make 8-inch circles about ¼ inch thick, using the marks on the baking sheet as guides. Smooth the meringue. Bake the meringue disks for 40 minutes. Remove them from the oven, and let them cool. Gently peel the waxed paper from the three meringue circles, and let them dry.

Melt the chocolate in 3 tablespoons of water.

Whip the cream until it is stiff. Add ⅓ cup of sugar to the cream, and beat until the cream is very stiff.

Place one circle of meringue on a cake plate. Spread the chocolate thinly and gently over it. Add a layer of sliced strawberries and cover with a layer of whipped cream. Put the second circle of meringue on top of the whipped cream, and again cover with chocolate, strawberries, and whipped cream. Add the third meringue circle, and cover the entire cake with the remaining whipped cream. Refrigerate for 3 hours before serving.

Slice with a warm wet knife.

Serves 6.

GALATOIRE'S

209 Bourbon Street

Jean Galatoire opened a hotel and restaurant in Birmingham, Alabama, in 1895. From there he moved to the Chicago World's Fair. In 1905, he opened Galatoire's on Bourbon Street. It is in the same location today. Jean's nephews Justin, Leon, and Gabriel came from France to help their uncle with the business. When he retired in 1916, they bought the thriving restaurant and continued its operation.

Galatoire's is truly a New Orleans retaurant. Everyone waits in line to be seated—no reservations are accepted—and the clientele at lunchtime is a veritable who's who of the local social and business worlds.

Justin's daughter Yvonne Galatoire Wynne has been involved with the daily management of the restaurant for over forty years. She is now assisted by fourth-generation members of the family, David Gooch, Justin Frey, and Leon Galatoire.

Exterior of Galatoire's.

Oysters en Brochette

18 strips of bacon, cut in half
3 doz. raw oysters
1 egg
¾ cup milk
1¼ cups flour
¼ tsp. salt (you may reduce this amount
   if oysters are salty)

¼ tsp. black pepper
oil for deep frying
6 toast points
6 lemon wedges

Fry the bacon until it is slightly browned, being careful not to overcook it because the bacon should be pliable.

Alternate six oysters and six half strips of bacon (folded) on each of six 8-inch skewers.

Make a batter by combining the egg and the milk.

Season the flour in a pan with the salt and pepper.

Dip each skewer in the batter and roll in the flour.

Deep-fry the oysters and bacon in hot oil until they are golden brown.

Serve on toast points with a lemon wedge.

Serves 6 as an appetizer.

Crabmeat Yvonne

1 lb. fresh mushrooms, washed and sliced
1 stick plus 2 tbs. butter, clarified
2 lbs. fresh backfin lump crabmeat
½ tsp. salt or to taste
¾ tsp. white pepper or to taste

6 fresh boiled, sliced artichoke bottoms
8 toast points
8 tbs. finely chopped parsley
8 lemon wedges

In a large skillet, sauté the mushrooms in the clarified butter for 10–15 minutes or until the mushroom liquid is reduced to a thick sauce. Add the crabmeat, and season with the salt and pepper. Then add the sliced artichoke bottoms, and sauté gently until thoroughly heated.

Serve over toast points, garnishing the plates with parsley and lemon wedges.

Serves 6.

Godchaux Salad

1 head iceberg lettuce, cored and cubed
2 large tomatoes, stems removed, cubed
1 lb. backfin lump crabmeat
30–35 large shrimp, boiled and peeled
⅔ cup salad oil

⅔ cup red wine vinegar
½ cup Creole mustard
3 hard-boiled eggs
12 anchovies

In a large salad bowl combine the lettuce, tomatoes, crabmeat, and shrimp.

In a small bowl, combine the oil, vinegar, and mustard, mixing well with a wire whisk. Pour the dressing over the salad, and toss.

Divide the salad onto six chilled plates (approximately 2 cups each). Garnish each salad with ½ of a sieved hard-boiled egg and 2 anchovies.

Serves 6 as an entrée.

Clockwise from top: Godchaux Salad, Crabmeat Yvonne, Crêpes Maison, Oysters en Brochette.

Crêpes Maison

Crêpes:
- ¾ cup flour
- 2 tsp. sugar
- ½ tsp. salt
- 3 eggs
- ¾ cup milk
- 1 tbs. butter, melted

Filling:
- 12 tbs. (6 oz.) currant jelly
- 3 tbs. sifted powdered sugar
- ½ cup sliced almonds
- ¼ cup Triple Sec

To make the crêpes, sift the flour, sugar, and salt together in a bowl. In a small mixing bowl, beat the eggs. Add the milk and then the dry ingredients, and beat the batter in a mixer on medium speed or blend in a blender until the batter is smooth. Allow the batter to sit for about 1 hour before cooking.

Heat a 6-inch crêpe pan over medium-high heat. Lift the pan from the heat, and, using a pastry brush, brush the bottom of the pan lightly with a little melted butter. Premeasure 2 tablespoons of batter, and pour the batter into the middle of the pan. Quickly tilt the pan so that the batter spreads evenly over the bottom. Return the pan to the heat, and brown the crêpe lightly. Turn the crêpe with a spatula, and brown the other side. Repeat the above process until all the batter is used, brushing the pan with melted butter as needed. Place the crêpes (there will be 12–16 of them) on layers of waxed paper until they are ready to fill.

Spread 1 tablespoon of jelly on each crêpe. Fold the crêpes into thirds. Place them side by side in an oblong baking pan. Sprinkle the crêpes with powdered sugar, and top them with sliced almonds. Place the crêpes under the broiler for 3–5 minutes or until the almonds are lightly toasted. Remove the crêpes from the heat, and sprinkle Triple Sec over them.

Allow 2 crêpes per serving.

Serves 6–8.

KOLB'S

125 St. Charles Avenue

Founded in 1899 by Conrad Kolb, this restaurant serves an unusual combination of German and Creole cuisines. Kolb's has remained and flourished in the same location since its inception. The building, a New Orleans landmark, was the site of the original Louisiana Jockey Club in 1845.

The aim of Kolb's has always been to serve the finest foods in an atmosphere dedicated to good dining.

The restaurant contains authentic German dark wood paneling and an intricate system of fans in the Grill. These ceiling fans were especially manufactured for the Exhibit Hall of the Cotton Centennial in 1884. They were then—and still are—marveled at by thousands as the forerunners of air conditioning.

The new owners, along with general manager Peter Ferroe, are dedicated to preserving the heritage of Kolb's.

Borscht

2 quarts water	1 tbs. tomato paste
3 large beets, peeled and grated	1/2 tsp. sugar
grated peel from 1/2 lemon	1 1/2 tsp. salt
2 medium onions, finely chopped	2 eggs, lightly beaten
1 cup tomato purée	3/4 cup sour cream

In a soup pot bring the water to a boil. Add the beets, lemon peel, and onions. Simmer for 1 hour. Add the tomato purée and tomato paste, and cook gently for 30 minutes. Add the sugar and salt, and blend thoroughly. Add 1 cup of the hot borscht to the beaten eggs, stirring constantly. Pour this mixture back into the borscht pot.

Serve hot, topping each portion with 1 tablespoon of sour cream.

Borscht can also be served cold. You may, however, need to adjust the seasonings.

Serves 8.

Oysters Kolb's

Hollandaise Sauce:
    12 egg yolks (room temperature)
    ½ cup fresh lemon juice
    1 tsp. salt
    ¼ tsp. cayenne
    4 sticks butter
36 fresh, medium-sized oysters in shells
rock salt

¼ cup clarified butter
¼ tsp. finely minced garlic
1 lb. lump crabmeat
1 tbs. finely chopped green onions
¼ cup sherry
salt to taste
white pepper to taste

To make the hollandaise, combine in a blender the egg yolks, lemon juice, salt, and cayenne. Blend the mixture at high speed for 30 seconds.

Heat 4 sticks of butter until the butter starts to bubble, being careful not to brown it. With the blender on high speed, add the butter in a slow, steady stream until all the ingredients are well blended. Transfer the sauce to the top of a double boiler, and cook over low heat, whisking constantly until it is thickened. Remove the hollandaise from the heat. (The sauce will become lumpy, or it may separate if cooked too long or at too high a temperature.)

Preheat the oven to 375 degrees.

Shuck the oysters, reserving the bottom shells, and drain them, but do not rinse them. Place the oysters on the bottom shells and arrange them on a bed of rock salt in two large shallow pans or six pie pans.

Pour the clarified butter into a large skillet, and heat it until it becomes bubbling hot. Add the garlic, and stir to distribute it around the pan. Add the crabmeat, and sauté the ingredients until the crabmeat is evenly heated (5–8 minutes). Then add the green onions, sherry, salt, and pepper, and sauté the mixture for a few minutes more until all the ingredients are well blended.

Meanwhile, place the pans of oysters in the preheated oven, and cook them for 10 minutes. Remove them from the heat. Spoon a well-rounded tablespoon of the crabmeat mixture over each oyster. Top this combination with 1½ tablespoons of hollandaise sauce to cover the oyster. Broil the oysters under a medium flame until the hollandaise lightly browns. Serve immediately.

Serves 6.

Cucumber and Mushroom Salad
with House Dressing

House Dressing:
  1 cup Creole mustard
  ¼ cup tarragon vinegar
  ¼ cup salad oil
  1 tbs. sugar

¼ cup water
2 tbs. lemon juice
1 medium head iceberg lettuce
1 large cucumber
10–12 medium-sized mushrooms

To make the house dressing, combine the mustard, vinegar, oil, sugar, water, and lemon juice in a blender, and blend for 3 minutes. Refrigerate the dressing for at least 2 hours before serving.

Wash and drain the head of lettuce. Remove 6 whole outer leaves, and set them aside. Tear or chop the remainder of the lettuce.

Wash the cucumber, and slice thinly.

Trim, wash, and slice the mushrooms.

Line each of six salad bowls with an outer leaf of lettuce to form a "lettuce cup." Place approximately 1 cup of chopped lettuce into each lettuce cup. Evenly divide cucumber slices among the lettuce cups, placing them in a ring around the chopped lettuce. Top the chopped lettuce with the mushroom slices. Serve each salad with approximately ⅓ cup of the house dressing.

Serves 6.

Borscht with Pumpernickel and Rye Bread and Sour Cream.

Kaiser Schnitzel

Veal Stock:
    1 lb. veal trimmings and bones
    1 tbs. butter
    2 medium onions, diced
    2 medium carrots, diced
    2 celery tops
    1 bay leaf
    3–4 parsley sprigs
    1 cup dry white wine
    3 cups water
½ stick (4 tbs.) butter
4 tbs. flour

½ lb. raw peeled and deveined small
    shrimp
½ cup half-and-half
6 2-oz. cutlets of milk-fed veal, flattened
6 2-oz. cutlets of pork loin, flattened
¼ tsp. salt
⅛ tsp. white pepper
¾ cup all-purpose flour
2 eggs, beaten with ½ cup water
1 cup plain bread crumbs
2 sticks butter

To make the veal stock, brown the veal trimmings and bones in 1 tablespoon of butter. Add the diced onions and carrots, and sauté for 4–5 minutes. Add the celery tops, bay leaf, parsley, and wine, and reduce the liquid by half. Add the water, and simmer the stock for 1 hour. Strain. Reserve.

Make a roux by melting 4 tablespoons of butter in a saucepan and adding the flour. Cook, stirring constantly, over medium-low heat until the roux is medium brown in color, approximately 15 minutes. Slowly add 2 cups veal stock, and cook 2–3 minutes. Add the raw shrimp and simmer for 10 minutes. Add the half-and-half, and season with salt and pepper. Do not boil the sauce once the half-and-half has been added.

To prepare the cutlets, first sprinkle them with salt and pepper. Keep the veal cutlets separate from the pork cutlets. Dredge the veal cutlets in flour, then dip them in the egg-water mixture, and finally coat them with bread crumbs. In a large frying pan melt one stick of butter, and sauté the veal cutlets until they are golden brown. Follow the same procedure for the pork cutlets, using another stick of butter for sautéeing.

Place one of each cutlet on serving plates, and cover with the warm sauce.

Serves 6.

Clockwise from top: Borscht, Pumpernickel Bread Pudding, Kaiser Schnitzel, Cucumber and Mushroom Salad, Oysters Kolb's.

Pumpernickel Bread Pudding
with Whiskey Sauce

4 oz. pumpernickel bread, diced into
  $\frac{1}{4}$-inch cubes
4 oz. stale French bread, diced into
  $\frac{1}{2}$-inch cubes
$\frac{1}{3}$ cup walnuts, halved or large pieces
$\frac{1}{3}$ cup dark raisins, presoaked in hot
  water for 15–20 minutes
1$\frac{1}{2}$ cups milk
$\frac{1}{2}$ cup sugar
$\frac{1}{2}$ tsp. vanilla

$\frac{1}{4}$ tsp. nutmeg
dash of salt
3 eggs, well beaten
Whiskey Sauce:
  $\frac{1}{2}$ cup milk
  $\frac{1}{2}$ cup heavy cream
  $\frac{1}{4}$ tsp. vanilla
  $\frac{1}{4}$ cup sugar
  3 large egg yolks
  2 tbs. whiskey or rum

Combine the breads, walnuts, and drained raisins.

Scald 1$\frac{1}{2}$ cups of milk, and add $\frac{1}{2}$ cup of sugar, $\frac{1}{2}$ teaspoon of vanilla, the nutmeg, and the salt. Remove the milk mixture from the heat, and cool for 10 minutes. Beat the eggs into the milk mixture, and pour over the bread mixture. Allow the pudding to stand and soak for 30 minutes.

Grease a loaf pan or an 8 inch by 12 inch pan. Pour the mixture into the pan, and cover it for baking. Place the pan in a larger pan of water. Bake the pudding at 375 degrees for approximately 40 minutes. A knife inserted in the pudding should come out clean.

While the bread pudding is baking, make the whiskey sauce. Combine $\frac{1}{2}$ cup of milk, the cream, and $\frac{1}{4}$ teaspoon of vanilla, and scald. Remove the mixture from the heat, and cool slightly.

In the top of a double boiler, combine $\frac{1}{4}$ cup of sugar and the yolks. Heat this over low heat, whisking until the sugar dissolves. Add the milk mixture slowly to the yolk mixture, whisking constantly. Continue cooking until the sauce has thickened, approximately 15 minutes. Add the whiskey or rum.

Serve the pudding hot or warm with 3 tablespoons whiskey sauce per serving.

Serves 6.

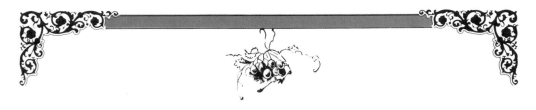

K-PAUL'S LOUISIANA KITCHEN

416 Chartres Street

The amazing success that Paul Prudhomme has achieved is a result of hard work and confidence in his own sense of taste.

Coming from a large family in Opelousas, Louisiana, Paul is one of our true Cajun restaurateurs in New Orleans. Paul's food is unusual in that rather than being French influenced by Creole, it is Cajun influenced by French. The result is very popular.

Paul's experience in New Orleans has been varied. He has assisted in opening several restaurants—the Bon Creole in the Madison Dupuy Hotel and Jack DuArte's Le Bistro. He helped the Brennans to achieve the high standards they demand in the Commander's Palace kitchen and, more recently, in their new restaurant, Mr. B's. He has taught cooking and has a regular local morning television show.

A few years ago, Paul's friend Kay Hindrichs, now Mrs. Paul Prudhomme, suggested they go into business on their own. Shortly thereafter, Kay and Paul purchased the building on Chartres Street known now as K-Paul's.

The success of the restaurant was quickly recognizable by the line in front in which one must wait for a table at both lunch and dinner. An added upstairs grocery offers many pâtés, breads, smoked meats, pickles, and sweets, all with a hint of Prudhomme's flair for Louisiana country cuisine. Plans for the future include dining-room expansion and a club dining room "for members only." There is also a cookbook in the works which should be available in the spring of 1983. The following recipes will be included in that work.

Seafood Dirty Rice

2 cups cold water
shrimp heads and shells from shrimp
  (below)
Dirty Rice:
    3 cups raw rice, converted or similar type
    5 cups chicken stock
    3 tbs. celery, chopped in ⅛-inch pieces
    3 tbs. onions, chopped in ⅛-inch pieces
    3 tbs. green bell pepper, chopped in
      ⅛-inch pieces
    3 tbs. margarine
    1 tsp. salt
    ¼ tsp. garlic powder
    pinch of ground red pepper, preferably
      cayenne
    pinch of black pepper
    pinch of white pepper
1 tbs. vegetable oil
2 tbs. unsalted butter
1 clove garlic, thinly sliced

¼ tsp. minced fresh garlic
2 tbs. celery, chopped in ⅛-inch pieces
2 tbs. onion, chopped in ⅛-inch pieces
2½ tbs. green bell pepper, chopped in
  ⅛-inch pieces
1 tsp. salt
½ tsp. ground red pepper, preferably
  cayenne
1 tsp. dried thyme
1 tsp. white pepper
½ cup crushed tomatoes in tomato purée
½ cup heavy cream
1¾ lbs. shrimp with heads and shells
  (sized 36–40 shrimp per pound;
  reserve the heads and shells to make
  shrimp stock)
1 packed cup (6 oz.) lump crabmeat
¾ cup green onions, very finely chopped

To make the shrimp stock, place the cold tap water and the shrimp heads and shells in a 1-quart saucepan. Bring this to a boil uncovered, and simmer uncovered over low heat for 30 minutes, adding water as necessary to maintain 1½ cups of stock in the pan. Strain. Cool and refrigerate the stock if it is not to be used immediately.

To make the dirty rice, in a 3-quart baking pan combine the raw rice, chicken stock, 3 tablespoons of celery, 3 tablespoons of onion, 3 tablespoons of bell pepper, margarine, 1 teaspoon of salt, garlic powder, a pinch of red pepper, black pepper, and a pinch of white pepper until they are well mixed. Seal the pan with aluminum foil. Bake the rice in a 350-degree oven until it is tender, about 1 hour.

Midway through the cooking of the rice, in a 9-inch skillet melt together the vegetable oil and butter. Add the garlic slices, minced garlic, 2 tablespoons of celery, 2 table-spoons of onion, 2½ tablespoons of bell pepper, 1 teaspoon of salt, ½ teaspoon of red pepper, thyme, white pepper, and crushed tomatoes. Sauté the mixture over medium heat for 5 minutes, stirring frequently. Add the 1½ cups of reserved shrimp

Chef Paul Prudhomme preparing blackened redfish.

stock, and continue cooking the mixture uncovered over high heat, stirring occasionally, for 10 minutes. Stir in the heavy cream, and simmer for 4 minutes. Add the peeled shrimp, and simmer, stirring occasionally, for 3 minutes. Stir in the crabmeat, green onions, and cooked rice. Simmer until all the ingredients are thoroughly heated. Serve immediately over 2 cups of dirty rice per portion.

Serves 6.

Southern Biscuit Muffins

2½ cups flour
¼ cup sugar
¼ tsp. salt
1½ tsp. baking powder

½ cup (1 stick) plus 2 tbs. unsalted butter,
    softened
1 cup milk

Mix the dry ingredients well in a mixing bowl. Work the butter in with your hands until it looks like corn meal, making sure you leave no lumps. Gradually add the milk, being careful not to overbeat as you stir it in with a spoon. Use enough milk so that the batter is wet but not runny. Spoon into a greased 12-cup muffin pan. Bake in a preheated oven at 350 degrees for 35–45 minutes or until golden brown.

Yield: 12 muffins.

Veal New Iberia

Crêpes:
 2 eggs
 1 1/2 tbs. vegetable oil
 1 cup milk
 1 tsp. sugar
 pinch of salt
 1/4 tsp. nutmeg
 3/4 cups plus 1 tbs. sifted flour
 vegetable oil for the crêpe pan
Roux:
 1/4 cup butter, preferably unsalted
 1/4 cup flour
New Iberia Sauce:
 2 cups chicken stock
 2 tbs. butter, preferably unsalted
 4 oz. tasso (a Louisiana cured smoked
  beef), diced into 3/4-inch pieces
 2 tbs. yellow onion, puréed
 1/4 tsp. minced fresh garlic
 1/2 tsp. salt
 1/2 tsp. black pepper
 pinch of powdered garlic, optional
 1 tsp. Tabasco
 1 green onion (top and bottom), chopped
  fine

1 1/2 cups sliced fresh mushrooms
1/2 cup butter, preferably unsalted
1/2 cup heavy cream
Hollandaise Sauce:
 2 egg yolks
 1/8 tsp. salt
 1/8 tsp. Tabasco
 1/2 tsp. lemon juice
 1/8 tsp. white vinegar
 1/2 tsp. white wine, plus additional wine to
  thin the sauce
 2 sticks butter, clarified
6 3-oz. pieces of white veal, pounded
 evenly to 1/4-inch thickness
salt, to taste
pepper, to taste
6 oz. Jarlsberg cheese, sliced 1/8 inch
 thick
flour, to dust the veal
1 tbs. butter, preferably unsalted
chopped parsley and/or sweet paprika

Make the crêpes. In a medium-sized mixing bowl whisk all the ingredients together, except the flour and the oil for the crêpe pan, only just enough to mix. Then add the flour, and, again, whisk just enough to mix—do not overbeat. Very lightly oil an 8 1/2-inch, slope-sided crêpe pan, and then wipe it with a towel until the pan has only enough oil on it to be shiny. Heat the pan over medium heat for about 2 minutes or until a drop of batter sizzles as soon as it is placed in the pan. Pick up the pan and slant it away from you. Pour 1/8 cup of batter into the pan, quickly rolling the batter so it coats the bottom and slightly up the sides of the pan. Make the crêpe as thin as possible. Cook about 1 1/2–2 minutes, or until the edges and underside of the crêpe are golden brown. Only brown one side of the crêpe. Remove the crêpe from the pan, and place it on a plate to cool, browned side up. Heat the pan about 30 seconds between the cooking of each crêpe, and make each crêpe as described above (you may need to reoil the pan once during the cooking process). Keep the crêpes at room temperature covered with a damp cloth until you are ready to use them (they should be used within two hours).

Yield: 12 crêpes, each about 6½ inches in diameter. There will be enough additional batter for two practice crêpes.

Note: You may make the batter ahead of time and refrigerate it. Allow it to return to room temperature before using.

Make the roux. In a 1-quart saucepan melt the butter over medium heat. Add the flour. Turn the flame to low, and whisk the roux for 1 minute. Remove the roux from the heat, and set it aside.

To make the New Iberia Sauce, bring the chicken stock to a boil in a 9-inch skillet. Lower the heat, and gently simmer until the stock is reduced to 1 cup.

In a separate skillet melt 2 tablespoons of butter over medium heat. Add the tasso, puréed onion, and minced garlic, and cook uncovered, stirring frequently and scraping the pan bottom well, until the tasso is browned and the onion is cooked (about 5 minutes). Add the reduced stock to the tasso, onion, and garlic and stir. Then stir in the salt, black pepper, powdered garlic, and Tabasco. Turn the heat up to high. When the tasso mixture is boiling, stir in the roux until the mixture becomes smooth. Reduce the heat to very low and continue simmering for 5 minutes, stirring constantly. Stir in the chopped green onion and mushrooms and ½ cup of butter (a few small chunks at a time). Continue stirring. When the butter is melted, stir in the heavy cream and bring to a boil. Remove the sauce from the heat, and reserve. (If the sauce is reheated before serving, do not heat too long or at too high a heat since the sauce will separate.)

Make the hollandaise sauce. In a small mixing bowl, add the egg yolks, salt, Tabasco, lemon juice, vinegar, and ½ teaspoon white wine. Mix the ingredients together with a whisk.

Skim the foam off the top of the clarified butter, then ladle the oil of the butter (not the thinner watery liquid on the bottom) into a bowl and reserve.

Boil some water in the bottom of a double boiler. Whisk the egg mixture on the top of the double boiler, over medium heat, making sure the bottom of the egg bowl does not touch the boiling water. Whip the eggs vigorously until they are thick and foamy

⟶

but not scrambled (about 1–1 ½ minutes). Remove the bowl from the heat. Gradually add the clarified butter in a thin stream while vigorously whipping the sauce. Make sure the butter you add is incorporated into the sauce before adding more. If the sauce gets too thick, it will break up. It should be runny, not like thick batter. Thin with 1 teaspoon of white wine, as needed.

To sauté the veal, season the veal with salt and pepper to taste. Lightly flour the veal. In a 9-inch skillet, melt 1 tablespoon of butter over medium heat until the foam disappears. Sauté the veal in the butter until the veal is browned on both sides (1–1 ½ minutes per side).

To serve, preheat the oven to 350 degrees.

Allow 1 crêpe per person. Lay the crêpe on a plate. Put 2 tablespoons of New Iberia Sauce into the center of the crêpe. Place the browned veal on top of the sauce, and neatly fold the crêpe in half, making sure the veal and sauce are not showing. Top the crêpe with 3 tablespoons more of New Iberia Sauce, and then ⅙ (1 ounce) of the sliced cheese. Place the crêpes in the oven (or under the broiler) until the cheese starts to melt. Remove from the oven. Top the crêpes with 2 tablespoons of hollandaise sauce, and sprinkle with chopped parsley and/or paprika. Serve immediately, with a fresh vegetable.

Serves 6.

Chef Paul Prudhomme.

Sweet Potato–Pecan Pie

3 medium-sized sweet potatoes (about
  8 oz. each)

Pie Dough:
  3 tbs. unsalted butter, softened
  2 tbs. sugar
  1/4 tbs. salt
  1/2 beaten egg (reserve the other half for
    the sweet-potato filling)
  2 tbs. milk
  1 cup flour

Pecan Pie Syrup:
  3/4 cup sugar
  2 eggs
  3/4 cup dark corn syrup
  1 1/2 tbs. unsalted butter, melted
  pinch of salt
  pinch of cinnamon
  3/4 tbs. vanilla extract

Sweet-Potato Filling:
  1 cup sweet-potato pulp, cooked
  1 tbs. unsalted butter, softened
  1/4 cup light brown sugar
  1 tbs. vanilla extract
  1/4 tsp. cinnamon
  1/8 tsp. nutmeg
  1/8 tsp. allspice
  1/4 tsp. salt
  1/2 beaten egg
  2 tbs. sugar
  1 tbs. heavy cream

1/2 cup pecans, pieces or halves

Chantilly Cream:
  3/4 cup heavy cream
  1 tbs. plus 2 tsp. sugar, or to taste
  1 tsp. Grand Marnier
  1 tsp. cognac

To bake the sweet potatoes, preheat the oven to 375 degrees. Place the sweet potatoes on a greased pan, and bake in the oven for 1 1/2 hours. Cool them (to speed up
the process, cut them in half). Remove the potato pulp with a spoon, and reserve the
pulp.

While the potatoes are baking, make the dough. Using an electric mixer with a
dough paddle on high speed or a food processor, combine the butter, sugar, and salt
until the mixture is creamy. Add the 1/2 egg, and beat for 30 seconds. Add the milk.
Beat on high speed until the batter is light and creamy and it sticks to the sides of the
bowl (about 2 minutes). Add the flour. Mix on medium speed for 5 seconds, then on
high speed for 5 seconds (overmixing will produce a tough dough). Remove the
dough from the bowl, and mold it by hand into a 5-inch-diameter patty that is 1/2 inch
thick. Lightly dust the patty with flour, and refrigerate it for a minimum of 1 hour,
preferably overnight. (The dough will last up to one week refrigerated.)

To make the pecan-pie syrup, place all the ingredients in the bowl of an electric
mixer. Mix thoroughly at slow speed until the mixture is opaque (about 1 minute).
Reserve.   →

To make the sweet-potato filling, place all the ingredients in the bowl of an electric mixer. Mix at medium speed until the batter is smooth (about 2–3 minutes). Do not overbeat.

On a floured cutting board roll out the patty of dough to a thickness of $1/8$ to $1/4$ inch. Very lightly flour the top of the dough, and fold it into quarters. Carefully pick it up, and place it in a greased and floured 8-inch cake pan (or a pie pan with 2-inch sides) so that the corner of the folded dough is centered in the pan. Unfold the dough, and firmly press it to fit snugly along the sides and bottom of the pan. Refrigerate the crust for 15 minutes.

To assemble the pie, preheat the oven to 325 degrees. Spoon the sweet-potato filling on top of the pie dough, and smooth the surface to make it level. Sprinkle the pecans evenly over the top of the sweet-potato filling. Then pour the pecan syrup on top, filling the pan to $1/4$ inch from the top to allow the pie room to rise as it bakes. Bake the pie for $1^3/4$ hours or until a knife inserted into the pie's center comes out clean. For a browner crust, after the first hour bake the pie on the lowest oven rack. (*Note:* The pecans will rise to the top of the pie during baking.) Cool. This pie keeps best at room temperature for the first 24 hours. After 24 hours it should be refrigerated.

To make the Chantilly Cream, refrigerate a medium-size mixing bowl and electric-mixer beaters until they are very cold. Place the heavy cream and sugar in the bowl, and beat with an electric mixer on low to medium speed until the cream is frothy (about 30 seconds). Turn the mixer up to high, and beat the cream until its consistency is thick and soft peaks form (about $1^1/2$ minutes). Do not overbeat. Add the Grand Marnier and cognac, and beat on high speed just until the liquids are thoroughly mixed into the cream (about 30 seconds).

Note: Be careful not to overbeat or the cream will become grainy, which is the first step in the cream becoming butter. Once it becomes grainy, you cannot return it to its former consistency. (But if this ever happens, enjoy it on toast!)

Serve the pie topped with Chantilly Cream.

Serves 6.

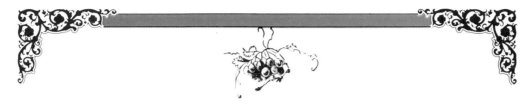

LA LOUISIANE

725 Iberville Street

Louis Bezaudun opened a restaurant in 1835 called the Crystal Dining Room. When in 1881 he married Mlle. Freyss, sister-in-law to Antoine Alciatore, founder of Antoine's, Bezaudun renamed his establishment the Hôtel et Restaurant de la Louisiane. La Louisiane served unusual French and Creole specialties and soon became a rendezvous for fashionable society. Under the guidance of Bezaudun's nephew Fernand Alciatore, the restaurant gained international prominence for gastronomic excellence. Alciatore's son Fernand Jr. carried on that tradition for another generation.

When Fernand Jr. died, La Louisiane was purchased by Omar Cheer, owner of the legendary Solari's Grocery. The ownership was then passed on to the Edward Seiler family and, in the 1930s, to "Diamond" Jim Moran. The next generation of Morans, Jimmy and Tony, continued to enhance the reputation of La Louisiane. A few years ago the restaurant was sold to Joseph Marcello, Jr. and Nick Mosca, both well-known local restaurateurs.

A total renovation and infusion of new blood are now bringing to La Louisiane the greatest success of its colorful history.

Cappelo di Angelo

3 tbs. butter
2½ cups finely chopped broccoli
3 cups finely chopped cauliflower
2 cups finely chopped green onions (with tops)
2 oz. pimiento, drained and diced
½ cup diced green pepper
1 cup chopped yellow onions
½ cup minced parsley
1 tsp. minced garlic
¼ lb. prosciutto, julienned
½ tsp. orégano

1 tsp. sweet basil
1¼ tsp. salt
¾ tsp. pepper
1 quart water
1 tbs. corn starch dissolved in 1 tbs. water
1 lb. angel hair or capellini or the thinnest pasta available, cooked according to package directions
Parmesan or Romano cheese, grated
pepper to taste

Melt the butter in a large skillet, and sauté all the vegetables and prosciutto lightly, about 3–5 minutes. Add the orégano, basil, salt, and pepper. Pour in the water, and simmer gently for 20–25 minutes. Stir in the corn starch. Let the sauce come to a boil, and remove from the heat.

Serve 1 cup of sauce (salsa primavera) over each portion of cooked pasta. Sprinkle with grated cheese and pepper to taste.

Serves 6.

Raw Vegetable Salad and Creole Dressing

Creole Dressing:
    1 cup plus 2 tbs. vegetable oil
    2 tbs. wine vinegar
    2 tbs. lemon juice
    ½ cup Creole mustard
    1 tsp. Worcestershire sauce
6 lettuce leaves
1 cup coarsely chopped broccoli

1 cup coarsely chopped cauliflower
1 cup julienned carrots
1 cup julienned zucchini
1 cup diced green peppers
1 cup diced celery
salt to taste
pepper to taste

100

Make the Creole Dressing by combining well the vegetable oil, vinegar, lemon juice, Creole mustard, and Worcestershire sauce, and refrigerating the dressing until ready to use.

Line six salad plates with the lettuce leaves. Toss the vegetables with salt and pepper, and allow 1 cup mixed vegetables per plate. Top each salad with the Creole Dressing.

Serves 6.

Veal La Louisiane

Seafood Béchamel Sauce:
    4 tbs. butter
    4 tbs. flour
    1 1/2 cups milk
    1/2 cup heavy cream
    2 tbs. butter
    8 medium-sized mushrooms, sliced
    1/4 lb. peeled and deveined small shrimp
    1/4 lb. lump crabmeat

    1 tsp. salt
    1/8 tsp. white pepper
    dash of nutmeg
    2 tbs. Madeira
6 thin pieces of white veal, 4 oz. each
1 cup Italian seasoned bread crumbs
1 stick butter or 1/2 cup olive oil

To make the seafood béchamel sauce, melt 4 tablespoons of butter in a saucepan, and stir in the flour. Cook over medium heat for 2–3 minutes, stirring constantly. Gradually stir in the milk, and bring to a boil. Reduce the heat, and add the cream. Cook 1 minute longer, then remove the mixture from the heat.

In a small skillet melt 2 tablespoons of butter, and sauté the mushrooms and shrimp over medium heat for about 5 minutes. Add the crabmeat, and cook 2 minutes longer. Stir this mixture into the béchamel. Season the sauce with salt, pepper, and nutmeg. Stir in the Madeira.

Dredge the veal in bread crumbs. Heat either 1 stick of butter or 1/2 cup of olive oil in a large skillet, and pan-fry the veal until it is golden brown. Place the veal on serving dishes and top each piece with 1/3 cup of the seafood béchamel sauce.

Serves 6.

Clockwise from top right: Raw Vegetable Salad, Chocolate Cheesecake, Spinach Cake, Cappelo di Angelo, Veal La Louisiane.

Sautéed Spinach

3 10-oz. packages fresh spinach
3 garlic cloves, mashed
2½ tbs. olive oil

1 tsp. salt, or to taste
¼ tsp. pepper

Wash the spinach, and remove the stems. Drain the spinach thoroughly. Sauté the spinach and garlic in olive oil over medium heat for approximately 5 minutes or until tender. Remove the spinach from the heat, and season it with salt and pepper.

Serves 6.

Chocolate Cheesecake

Crust:
    1 1/2 cups graham cracker crumbs
    1 stick butter, melted
    3 tbs. sugar
Filling:
    3 8-oz. packages cream cheese at room
      temperature

1 lb. semisweet chocolate
1 cup sugar
3 egg yolks
1 stick butter, melted and cooled
1/2 tsp. orange extract

Preheat the oven to 450 degrees.

To make the crust, combine the graham cracker crumbs, 1 stick of melted butter, and 3 tablespoons of sugar thoroughly in a bowl. Transfer the crust mixture to a 9-inch springform pan, pressing the crumbs evenly onto the bottom and 1 inch up the sides of the pan.

To make the filling, put the cream cheese in a large mixing bowl. Melt the chocolate in the top of a double boiler, and add it to the cream cheese. Beat the mixture at medium speed with an electric mixer until it is creamed. Add 1 cup of sugar and beat the mixture until it is light and fluffy. Add the egg yolks to the mixture one at a time, beating after each addition. Blend in 1 stick of melted butter and the orange extract, and beat until all the ingredients are thoroughly combined.

Pour the entire mixture into the crumb-lined pan. Place the pan on a cookie sheet in the middle of the oven, and bake the cake for 15 minutes. Allow the cake to cool completely.

Refrigerate the cake for at least 12 hours before serving. Release the spring, and remove the sides of the pan. Slice and serve the cake.

Serves 10–12.

LA PROVENCE

Highway 190, 7 miles east of the Causeway
Lacombe, Louisiana

Chris Kerageorgiou, the son of Greek immigrants, was born in Port Saint Louis, Provence, France, in 1927. He began working in a bakery at the age of eight. At fifteen, he joined the French underground and remained with them until the end of World War II. It was difficult for Chris to find work because of discrimination against Greeks, but he soon began cooking on a ship that carried wine from North Africa to France. He cooked in the Merchant Marines until his ship made port in San Francisco. Chris jumped ship at San Francisco and worked at the Palace Hotel. He then moved to Bakersfield, Las Vegas, and finally New Orleans. He soon met his wife-to-be, who is from Louisiana. Chris made many moves in the restaurant community, learning what he could from each place. He cooked at the Jung Hotel, Sclafani's, the Vieux Carré Restaurant, Brennan's, and the Beverly. He then became chef at the newly constructed Royal Orleans Hotel. After twenty-two years at the Royal Orleans, Chris opened his own restaurant, La Provence, in Lacombe, Louisiana.

Chris is constantly testing and developing his cuisine, which tends toward lighter, less complicated fare. Chris maintains a fresh herb garden on the La Provence property and goes to great pains to acquire the best and freshest products. Their preparation is simple and excellent.

Clockwise from top right: Steamed Broccoli and Cauliflower, Suprêmes de Poulet aux Écrevisses, Crab Soup, Orange Mousse.

Steamed Crabmeat au Beurre Blanc

½ cup white wine
1½ tbs. finely chopped French shallots or
    white part of green onions
¼ cup heavy cream
3 sticks cold butter
1 tbs. chopped parsley

1 4-oz. jar pimientos, drained and diced
½ tsp. salt
¼ tsp. white pepper
1 tbs. sugar
1 lb. lump crabmeat

Place the white wine and shallots in a saucepan. Cook the mixture, reducing it by three-fourths. Add the cream, and reduce it over medium heat until it is thick. Cut the butter into small pieces. With a whisk slowly beat the butter into the cream over a low flame so that the butter does not separate. Whip until all the butter is incorporated into the cream and the sauce is smooth and creamy. Never let the beurre blanc come to a boil once you have begun adding the butter. Add the parsley, pimientos, and seasonings. (It is very important to serve this dish immediately after the beurre blanc is finished since the sauce will soon separate.)

Meanwhile lightly steam the crabmeat in a vegetable steamer until the crabmeat is warm, but not hot. Divide the crabmeat into 6 half-cup ramekins (approximately ⅓ cup of crabmeat per ramekin). Pour the beurre blanc over each portion.

Serves 6 as an appetizer.

Crab Soup

⅓ cup olive oil
2 leeks (white part only), cut into halves
    and thinly sliced crosswise
3 small carrots, thinly sliced
1⅓ cups diced onion (approximately
    1 medium onion)
1 tsp. pressed garlic
2 quarts fish stock
4 fresh uncooked crabs, top shells

removed, gills cleaned out, and cut into
quarters
2 cups diced tomatoes (approximately
    2 medium tomatoes)
½ cup finely chopped broad leaf parsley
⅛ tsp. powdered saffron or a healthy
    pinch saffron threads
¼ tsp. black pepper
salt to taste

In a large saucepan, heat the olive oil. Sauté the leeks, carrots, onion, and garlic very lightly (approximately 2 minutes). Add the fish stock, crabs, tomatoes, parsley, and saffron. Cook slowly for ½ hour. Before serving add the pepper. Check for salt.

Serves 6.

Chef/owner Kerageorgiou preparing his crab soup.

Suprêmes de Poulet aux Écrevisses

3 tbs. French shallots	6 chicken breasts, lightly floured
5 oz. white wine	12 oz. crawfish tails
3 pints (6 cups) chicken stock	½ tsp. salt
3 pints (6 cups) heavy cream	½ tsp. white pepper
3 tbs. cooking oil	parsley

Sauté the shallots in white wine, and reduce the liquid by half. Add the stock and cream. Simmer over low heat for 45 minutes to 1 hour until it has thickened.

In a sauté pan heat the oil. Sauté the lightly floured chicken breasts for approximately 15 minutes or until the meat is pink inside. Remove the chicken from the heat.

Just before serving add the crawfish to the sauce. Season with salt and pepper. Add the breasts, and cook them until they are done (5–10 minutes). Arrange the chicken on a platter or on dinner plates. Spoon the sauce over the chicken. Garnish with parsley.

Note: Your favorite herb or herb mixture may be added to the sauce, if desired.

Serves 6.

Steamed Broccoli and Cauliflower

1 head cauliflower	3 French shallots or 1 bunch green-onion
1 bunch broccoli	bulbs, finely chopped
1 stick butter	

Cut the cauliflower into small flowerettes, leaving only a small amount of the stem.

Cut the stems off the broccoli until only enough remains to hold the flowerettes in place.

Steam the vegetables lightly in a vegetable steamer so that they still maintain their color and crispness.

In a large saucepan, melt the butter, and sauté the shallots or green onions for 2–3 minutes. Add the steamed vegetables, and sauté for a few minutes until they are well coated with the butter and shallots or onions and are thoroughly heated.

Arrange the broccoli in a circle on a small vegetable platter with the cauliflower in the center.

Note: For a variation or additional color, carrot, green bean, or turnip slices can be added to the broccoli and cauliflower.

Serves 6.

Orange Mousse

6 egg yolks
1 orange, grated for zest and then juiced
1 lemon, grated for zest and then juiced
3 tbs. orange-juice concentrate mixed
   with 5 tbs. water

1 cup sugar
2 cups heavy cream
2 tbs. sugar

In a stainless-steel mixing bowl, beat the egg yolks. Add (a little bit at a time) the fresh lemon and orange juice and the orange-juice concentrate while whisking over low heat. Make sure to move the bowl in a circular motion so that the eggs will not scramble. Continue to beat and move the bowl until the eggs become slightly thick. Add 1 cup of sugar slowly while continuing to beat the mixture until it has thickened and the egg yolks taste cooked (approximately 20–30 minutes). Add the zest during the last few minutes of cooking. Set the mixture aside, and cool it.

Whip the cream to the soft-peak stage, and gradually add 2 tablespoons of sugar while beating.

When the yolk mixture feels cool, slowly fold in the whipped cream until it is well blended.

Spoon or, using a pastry bag, pipe the mousse into dessert glasses. Chill the mousse for several hours before serving.

Serves 6.

LERUTH'S

636 Franklin Avenue
Gretna, Louisiana

Warren LeRuth's work experiences are probably more varied than those of any other restaurateur in New Orleans. Born and raised in New Orleans, he practically grew up in his mother's kitchen, where the family spent most of its time. Early in his life he found that he had a keen interest in baking and landed his first job at Solari's, where a large amount of bread and pastries were prepared daily. From there it seems he never stopped moving.

Warren wanted to learn more about cooking, and talked Justin Galatoire into letting him help out in Galatoire's kitchen a few mornings and evenings without pay. He left Solari's and began working as a pastry chef in the Monteleone Hotel. He then left Galatoire's and got a second job at the Four Seasons Pastry Shop. Six months later he left the Monteleone and the Four Seasons and secured a full-time position as chef at the New Orleans Country Club. From here he moved to Texas and worked in several restaurants, then went back to New Orleans to the Jung Hotel and the Beverly. Warren then worked on ships—first as a deckhand, then as cook, and was General Clark's chef during the Korean conflict. Later he worked as a researcher for Procter & Gamble and then assisted in developing the Duncan Hines cake mixes. As a food researcher, Warren invented the emulsion which is used in almost every commercial salad dressing. Afterward, he opened a restaurant in Texas. He continued moving and learning and developing food products until the opening of LeRuth's Restaurant in 1966.

In the renovated raised Victorian cottage where he operates today, Warren LeRuth has built a reputation as one of the finest (to many, the pinnacle) of New Orleans' restaurateurs.

Warren's two sons began spending time in the kitchen as children just to see their dad more often. Lee was seven and Larry was nine. They used to stand on drink cases and cook on the ranges. Warren's wife Marie worked at the door for many years, greeting guests. The restaurant has prospered and enlarged through a concerted family effort.

Warren recently sold LeRuth's to his sons. With the help of their dad, Lee and Larry will continue one of the great restaurants of this city. Warren LeRuth says of this exchange, "There are two things a man can give to his children: one is roots; the other is wings."

Lump Crabmeat and Crawfish Cardinal

Béchamel Sauce:
    1/2 stick butter
    4 tbs. flour
    1 cup milk or fish stock
    1/2 cup cream
    1/2 tsp. salt or to taste
    1/8 tsp. white pepper
2 green onions, chopped fine
1/2 stick butter

1/4 cup white wine
1/4 cup tomato sauce
1/2 lb. lump crabmeat
1 lb. cooked and peeled crawfish tails
1/4 cup crawfish fat (if available)
1/4 tsp. salt
1/8 tsp. cayenne

To make the béchamel, melt 1/2 stick of butter in a saucepan, and stir in the flour. Cook the roux over medium heat for 1 minute. Add the milk or stock, and cook the sauce for approximately 5 minutes, stirring constantly. Add the cream, 1/2 teaspoon of salt, and white pepper. Cook the sauce for another 1/2 minute.

Sauté chopped onions in 1/2 stick of butter for 1 minute over medium-high heat. Add the white wine and tomato sauce, and cook the mixture over medium-low heat for 5 minutes. Add the béchamel sauce, and return the mixture to a boil. Add the crabmeat, crawfish, and fat. Return the mixture to a boil, stirring gently.

Serves 6.

Jean Paul's Sweetbreads Madeira

1½ lbs. cleaned veal sweetbreads
Brown Sauce:
    1½ sticks butter
    6 tbs. flour
    2 cups beef stock or bouillon
    ¼ tsp. salt, or to taste
    ¼ tsp. black pepper, or to taste

1 cup flour
1 tsp. salt
½ tsp. black pepper
2 eggs, lightly beaten
1 stick butter
½ cup Madeira

Blanch the sweetbreads in simmering water for approximately 10 minutes. Drain the sweetbreads, and allow them to cool.

Make the brown sauce by melting 1½ sticks of butter and stirring in 6 tablespoons of flour. Cook over low heat, stirring constantly, until the roux turns a medium brown (approximately 15–20 minutes). Add the stock or bouillon and salt and pepper to taste, depending on the seasonings in the stock.

Slice the cooled sweetbreads in half. Dip them in 1 cup of flour seasoned with 1 teaspoon of salt and ½ teaspoon of pepper and then in the eggs. Immediately sauté the sweetbreads in the stick of butter, and brown both sides.

Drain half the butter from the pan, and place the sweetbreads and remaining butter into a hot (475-degree) oven for 5 minutes. Drain the remaining butter.

Add half of the Madeira (¼ cup) and 1 cup of the brown sauce to the sweetbreads and bring to a boil. Pour in the remainder of the Madeira, heat, and flame. Add the rest of the brown sauce, heat, and serve.

Serves 6.

Bibb Lettuce and Mushroom Salad
with Vermouth Dressing

2 heads Boston lettuce
1 cup sliced fresh mushrooms

Dressing:
    ⅓ cup salad oil
    2 tbs. dry vermouth
    ¼ tsp. salt

Tear the cleaned lettuce into bite-size pieces. Arrange the sliced mushrooms over the lettuce.

Thoroughly mix the oil, vermouth, and salt, pour it over the vegetables, and gently toss the salad.

Note: LeRuth created this recipe for Les Amis du Vin because they wanted to have wine with salad without having the acidity from vinegar or lemon spoil the flavor of the delicate wine.

Serves 6.

Foreground, left to right: Lump Crabmeat and Crawfish Cardinal, Homemade Vanilla Ice Cream with Irma's Pecan Thins, Jean Paul's Sweetbreads Madeira, Romaine and Mushroom Salad.

LeRuth's Green Goddess Dressing

1 cup homemade mayonnaise
1 cup sour cream
½ cup heavy cream
2 tbs. chopped parsley
3 tbs. chopped green onion (green part only)

1 tsp. chopped garlic
1 tbs. anchovy paste
1 tsp. salt
½ tsp. white pepper

Combine all the ingredients in a blender, and blend until smooth.

Yield: 2⅓ cups.

Irma's Pecan Thins

1 stick butter, softened
½ cup brown sugar
½ cup white sugar
1 tsp. vanilla
½ cup chopped pecans

1½ cups sifted flour
¼ tsp. baking powder
¼ tsp. baking soda
1 small egg

Place all the ingredients in a bowl except the egg. Mix for 3–5 minutes by hand. When the ingredients begin to form a mass, add the egg and mix the dough to a smooth consistency. Shape the dough with your hands into a log measuring 1½ inches in diameter. Roll the log in wax paper, and chill it overnight.

Preheat the oven to 350-degrees.

Grease some cookie sheets.

Slice the cold cookie dough ⅛ inch thick, and place the cookies on the sheets, spacing them approximately 1 inch apart. Bake the cookies for about 12 minutes.

The cookies become crispy when cooled and will be too brittle to loosen from the pan unless you run a spatula under them while they are still warm.

Yield: approximately 40 cookies.

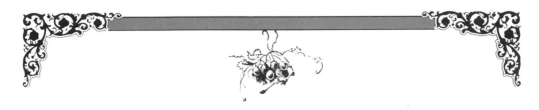

L'ESCALE

Saint Louis Hotel
730 Bienville Street

A truly spectacular addition to the list of New Orleans restaurants is L'Escale in the St. Louis Hotel. Conceived by hotelier/restaurateur Mark Smith, L'Escale brings to the city the ultimate in current French haute cuisine. The kitchen, presided over by Chef Philippe Dufau, specializes in producing major dining events with an eight-course table d'hôte menu. La Soirée Parisienne is a masterpiece of coordination in new and unusual dishes.

Fresh products flown in daily from France combined with Louisiana's own special reserves have been brought together to create a totally unique cuisine. This small forty-seat restaurant is one whose company we hope to keep for a long time to come.

Clockwise from right: Chocolate Soufflé, St. Jacques à la Mousse d'Avocats, Aiguillettes de Canard au Gingembre, Chausson d'Écrevisses aux Huitres.

115

St. Jacques à la Mousse d'Avocats
(Scallops with Avocado Mousse)

8 oz. scallops, sliced thinly
salt
white pepper
1 tbs. sesame seeds
3 large lemons, juiced
1 ripe avocado

1 tbs. cognac
1 tbs. red port
¼ tsp. salt
⅛ tsp. white pepper
1 cup heavy cream (very cold)
1 head of Boston lettuce

Season the sliced scallops lightly with salt and white pepper. Add the sesame seeds, and marinate the scallops in the lemon juice for 30 minutes.

To prepare the avocado mousse, peel the avocado and purée it. Mix in the cognac, port, salt, and pepper.

Whip the cream until stiff peaks form. Fold the avocado purée into the whipped cream.

For the presentation, slice the Boston lettuce and make a small bed of lettuce in the center of each of six plates. Top each lettuce bed with 2 heaping tablespoons of avocado mousse. Drain the scallops and arrange them overlapping the mousse. Around the bed of lettuce, decorate the plates with extra avocado and scallop slices. (Also use radish slices and a carrot julienne marinated in oil-and-vinegar dressing.)

Serves 6 as an appetizer.

Chausson d'Écrevisses aux Huitres
(Crawfish and Oysters Chausson)

12 oz. prepared puff pastry
1 egg yolk
1 tsp. water
1½ tbs. butter, melted
3 tbs. finely chopped French shallots
1½ doz. fresh oysters, drained
5½ oz. mussel meat

13½ oz. crawfish tails
1½ tbs. dry white wine
3 tbs. cognac
¾ cup fish stock
3 tbs. sliced green onions
6 tbs. very cold butter

Preheat the oven to 400 degrees.

On a lightly floured surface roll out the puff pastry to ¼-inch thickness. With a knife cut out 6 individual oval-shaped pastries, each measuring 5–6 inches long. Place them on an ungreased cookie sheet, and brush the tops with a wash made of the egg yolk beaten with the water. Bake the ovals in the oven for 15–20 minutes until golden brown. Cool the pastries slightly, then cut them in half horizontally, scooping out any layers of uncooked pastry. Set the pastries aside on six individual serving plates until you are ready to fill and serve them.

In a heavy skillet melt 1½ tablespoons of butter. Over low heat sauté the shallots for 2–3 minutes. Add the oysters, mussels, and crawfish tails, and sauté the seafood for 5 minutes. Add the wine, and simmer the mixture over medium-low heat for 1 minute. Pour in the cognac, and cook for 1 minute more. Add the fish stock, and while it is being heated, remove the seafood from the sauce with a slotted spoon and place it in a bowl with the green onions. By this time the sauce should be heated to a simmer. Remove the skillet from the heat. Add 6 tablespoons of cold butter to the hot sauce, and stir gently until it has melted. Fold the seafood and green onions into the sauce until they are well combined.

Spoon a generous ½ cup seafood with sauce into each pastry bottom and cover it with a pastry top. Serve immediately.

Serves 6.

Aiguillettes de Canard au Gingembre
(Ginger Duck)

½ cup finely chopped gingerroot
2 tbs. thinly sliced French shallots
2 tbs. butter
½ cup white wine
4 cups duck or veal stock
3 tbs. cornstarch mixed with 5–6 tbs.
   cool water to make a paste
½ cup red wine vinegar

½ cup granulated sugar
1 tbs. fresh lemon juice
6 duck breasts, boned (the bones from
   the duck can be used to make the
   stock, above)
salt
pepper
peanut oil

To make the ginger sauce, sauté in a medium saucepan the ginger and shallots in the butter over low heat for 3–4 minutes. Add the wine, and reduce the mixture until it is almost dry. Add the stock to the reduced ginger-shallot mixture, and cook it for 15 minutes, skimming frequently. Add the cornstarch paste, and, while stirring, bring the sauce to a boil. Strain the sauce to remove the ginger and shallots, and return the strained sauce to the saucepan. Do not cook it anymore at this point.

In another saucepan bring the vinegar and sugar to a boil. Simmer the mixture for about 15–20 minutes or just until it turns a rich caramel color. Remove the mixture immediately from the heat.

Bring the strained sauce back to a boil. Cautiously add it to the still hot caramel mixture by pouring it in a slow stream while stirring vigorously. Gently boil this mixture for 1 minute. Add the lemon juice.

Preheat the oven to 450 degrees.

Season the duck breasts with salt and pepper.

Heat a small amount of peanut oil in a skillet. Place the breasts skin side down into the hot oil. Place the breasts and oil in the oven, and cook them for 7–10 minutes. The duck will be rosy-colored on the inside.

Reheat the sauce. Place about 2–3 tablespoons of the sauce in the middle of each plate. Place thinly sliced duck in a fan-shaped pattern over the sauce.

Serves 6.

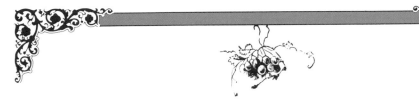

LOUIS XVI

Marie Antoinette Hotel
829 Toulouse Street

In 1969, when Mark Smith conceived the idea of building the Marie Antoinette Hotel in the Vieux Carré, he also imagined creating a true French restaurant. He wanted to produce something different than what was being done at Antoine's, Arnaud's, Brennan's, and other establishments. Louis XVI was born.

With the help of George Huber (who went on to open Romanoff's), Mark set out to find the right chef to run the kitchen. Daniel Bonnot was brought to the United States to do the job. As planned, Daniel produced a classic French menu for Louis XVI. Since that time, the inevitable has occurred—a touch of New Orleans and Creole cuisines has crept into Chef Bonnot's creations.

The food and service here are superb. Louis XVI stands as one of our most elegant restaurants.

Clockwise from top: Cream of Broccoli Soup, Crawfish Beignets, Lamb en Croûte, Strawberries Melba.

119

Cold hors d'oeuvres cart.

Crawfish Beignets with Tomato Sauce

Tomato Sauce:
- 1 cup finely diced white onion (approximately 1 large onion)
- 2 tbs. finely diced garlic (approximately 2 cloves)
- 1 tbs. butter
- $\frac{1}{2}$ cup chicken stock
- 1 bay leaf
- 6 whole ripe tomatoes, peeled, seeded, and diced
- 2 oz. tomato paste
- $\frac{1}{2}$ tsp. salt
- $\frac{1}{4}$ tsp. white pepper

Beignets:
- $1\frac{1}{2}$ cups flour
- 1 tbs. baking powder
- 2 green onions (white part only), finely sliced
- 2 oz. pimiento, finely chopped
- 1 clove garlic, finely chopped
- 1 cup water
- 1 tbs. olive oil
- 8 oz. cooked and peeled crawfish tails
- $\frac{3}{4}$ tsp. salt
- $\frac{1}{4}$ tsp. Tabasco
- oil for frying

To make the sauce, sauté the onion and garlic in butter over low heat until they become translucent (approximately 2–3 minutes). Add the chicken stock, bay leaf, tomatoes, and tomato paste. Cook the sauce 15 minutes over medium heat. Remove the bay leaf, and purée the sauce in a blender. Keep the sauce warm.

To make the beignets, mix the flour, baking powder, green onions, pimiento, garlic, water, olive oil, crawfish tails, salt, and Tabasco in a bowl. Cover the bowl with a damp towel, and set it aside in a warm place for 30 minutes. Mix again, and drop spoonfuls of the mixture into hot oil (about 370 degrees). Fry until the beignets are lightly browned on both sides. A cast-iron skillet works well.

The beignets can be served alone or with warm tomato sauce spooned over them.

Serves 6 (4 beignets apiece).

Cream of Broccoli Soup

2 cups white onions, thinly sliced
2 tbs. butter
4 cups broccoli (approximately 1 bunch), chopped (remove the dry, woody part of the stem)
2 tbs. flour

1 quart milk
1 cup potatoes, peeled and sliced
2¼ tsp. salt
½ tsp. white pepper
1 cup heavy cream

Sauté the onions in the butter for 2–3 minutes or until the onions are soft. Do not brown the onions. Add the broccoli, and cook it gently for 10 minutes. Sprinkle the flour over the vegetables, and stir the mixture. Add the milk, sliced potatoes, salt, and pepper, and cook the soup over low heat for 15–20 minutes. Avoid overcooking to preserve the bright green color of the broccoli. Purée the soup in a blender or processor. Put the soup back into a saucepan, add the cream, and adjust the salt and pepper. Reheat slowly, and serve.

Serves 6.

Lamb en Croûte

1 2-lb. rack of lamb
10 oz. fresh spinach, cleaned
6 tbs. butter
1 cup onions, finely chopped
¼ tsp. salt
⅛ tsp. white pepper
2 tbs. Pernod or Herbsaint
1½ cups (6 oz.) minced fresh mushrooms
¼ tsp. salt
⅛ tsp. white pepper
Special Sauce:
    ½ cup lamb fat
    1 carrot, sliced medium thin
    1 onion, coarsely chopped

2 celery ribs, coarsely chopped
½ cup dry white wine
1½ cups water
1 tbs. cornstarch, dissolved in 2 tbs. water
¼ cup mint jelly
1 tsp. garlic, minced
2 tbs. chopped mint leaves
1 tbs. chopped parsley
¼ tsp. salt
⅛ tsp. white pepper
¼ tsp. white vinegar
½ lb. puff pastry (frozen prepared puff pastry can be bought in the grocery)
1 egg, beaten

Preheat the oven to 425 degrees.

Roast the rack of lamb in the oven for 15 minutes (for medium rare). Cool the lamb, and refrigerate it.

Boil the spinach for 15 minutes. Drain it, and squeeze it out to remove the excess water. When the spinach is cool, chop it. Melt 4 tablespoons of butter in a skillet, and sauté the chopped spinach and onion for 15 minutes. Add ¼ teaspoon of salt and ⅛ teaspoon of white pepper. Stir in the Pernod. Cool the mixture, and refrigerate it.

Melt 2 tablespoons of butter in a skillet, and sauté the minced mushrooms for 2–3 minutes or until the water is cooked out of them. Season the mushrooms with ¼ teaspoon of salt and ⅛ teaspoon of white pepper. Cool the mixture, and refrigerate it.

Remove the lamb from the refrigerator, and trim off most of the fat. Reserve the trimmings for the Special Sauce.

To make the Special Sauce, melt the fat from the trimmings. Sauté the carrot, onion, and celery over medium high heat until they are cooked (approximately 15 minutes). The fat will be slightly browned. Add the wine and water, and cook the mixture over medium heat for 12–15 minutes until the liquid is reduced by half. Add the cornstarch mixture and the mint jelly. Stir the mixture until it is thoroughly mixed. Strain the mixture. To the strained liquid add the garlic, mint, parsley, ¼ teaspoon of salt, ⅛ teaspoon of white pepper, and vinegar. Reheat the sauce just before serving.

To assemble the Lamb en Croûte, roll the puff pastry to a thickness of ¼ inch—one and one-half times the dimensions of the lamb. Pack the spinach mixture onto the outside of the lamb (the fat side). It will be between ¼ inch and ½ inch thick. Place this side down onto the center of the puff pastry. Pack the mushroom mixture into the rib side of the lamb. Pull up the sides of the puff pastry to encase the lamb. Brush on the beaten egg, and seal the edges of the pastry together with your fingers. Flip the entire rack of lamb over, and place it in a baking dish. (If you are using the prepared puff pastry, use both sheets since one sheet will not be enough to wrap around the rack of lamb. Place one sheet on the bottom and the second sheet on top. Trim the top sheet, and wrap up the edges. Seal the pastry with the egg as directed, and flip the lamb over into a baking dish.) Decorate the top of the pastry with the design of your choice by using the remaining puff-pastry scraps. Brush the crust with egg. Refrigerate the lamb for at least 15 minutes before cooking.

Place in a preheated 400-degree oven for 30 minutes. (See Note.)

Remove the lamb from the oven, and slice it into appropriate portions. Serve the lamb with a spoonful of heated Special Sauce on the plate and a gravy boat of sauce on the side.

Note: Lamb en Croûte will retain heat inside the pastry shell. Thus, it continues to ''cook'' after its removal from the oven. If not served immediately, it will tend to be more ''medium'' than ''medium rare'' when sliced.

Serves 2.

Noon buffet.

Strawberries Melba

Melba Sauce:
  2 pints fresh raspberries
  1 tbs. unsalted butter
  ½ cup sugar
  ½ cup white wine
  ½ cup water
  ½ tsp. lemon juice

vanilla ice cream
fresh strawberries, cleaned and halved or
  quartered
slightly sweetened whipped cream
sliced roasted almonds
mint leaves (optional)

For the Melba sauce, in a saucepan sauté the raspberries in butter for 1 minute. Add the sugar, wine, water, and lemon juice. Cook the sauce over medium heat for approximately 30 minutes or until the sauce is reduced by two-thirds. Purée the sauce, and strain it through a sieve, mashing the sauce with the back of a spoon to extract all the liquid. Chill the Melba sauce.

To serve, place a scoop of ice cream in each of eight goblets and surround the ice cream with strawberries. Top this with 2 tablespoons of Melba sauce. Finish with whipped cream that has been piped from a star-tipped pastry bag. Garnish with almonds, additional strawberries, and mint leaves.

Serves 8.

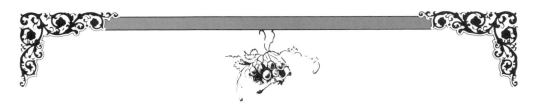

MAISON PIERRE

430 Dauphine Street

Pierre and Doralyn LaCoste have created one of New Orleans' most elegant restaurants. The fine china, crystal, and silver and the abundance of fresh flowers make you feel that you are dining in Paris.

The Maison Pierre offers a choice of à la carte or table d'hôte menus. The LaCostes' daughter Kipling has grown up in the restaurant and now oversees the dining room evenings.

Clockwise from right: Tournedos Andalouse, Black Bean Soup, Shrimp Mousquetaire, Café Pierre.

125

Shrimp Mousquetaire

6 large lettuce leaves
3 cups chopped lettuce
48 large boiled and peeled shrimp
Dressing:
    2 egg yolks
    $1/2$ tsp. salt
    $1/4$ tsp. white pepper
    $1/8$ tsp. cayenne
    $1/2$ tsp. Dijon mustard

$1/4$ cup lemon juice or more to taste
$1 1/4$ cups olive oil
1 tbs. boiling water
$1/4$ cup cold bouillon or consommé
2 tbs. chopped green onions (with tops)
$1/4$ cup white wine
1 tbs. chopped parsley
carrots for garnish

Place a lettuce leaf on each of six salad plates. Mound a $1/2$ cup of chopped lettuce in each leaf. Overlap 8 shrimp per serving over or around the chopped lettuce in an attractive manner.

For the dressing, beat the yolks, salt, pepper, cayenne, and mustard together to form a smooth paste. Add a little lemon juice, and then beat in one-fourth of the oil a little at a time. Add a little more lemon juice and then a little more oil as you continue to whisk. Add the rest of the oil in the same slow manner until the dressing is very thick. Beat in the boiling water. Add the cold bouillon by the tablespoon until the dressing is thinned to the consistency of sour cream.

In a small saucepan, simmer the green onions in the wine for 30 seconds. Remove the onions with a slotted spoon, and stir them into the dressing. Correct the seasonings (salt and cayenne will heighten the taste).

Coat the shrimp with the dressing, and serve the rest of the dressing on the side.

Garnish the salads with chopped parsley and with carrots, if desired.

Serves 6.

Black Bean Soup

1 lb. dried black beans	1 bay leaf
1½ lbs. salt pork	½ tsp. thyme leaves
12 cups water	2 tbs. dry sherry
1 cup chopped onions	salt to taste
1 cup chopped carrots	pepper to taste
1 cup chopped tomatoes	1 chopped hard-boiled egg
2 cloves chopped garlic	2 tbs. chopped parsley

Rinse and soak the beans in water to cover for 5–6 hours.

In a covered soup pot simmer the salt pork in the 12 cups of water until tender, about 1 hour. Remove the pork, and set it aside. Drain the beans, and add them to the pork broth along with the onions, carrots, tomatoes, and garlic. Tie the bay leaf and thyme in some cheese cloth, and add this to the pot. Cook the soup over low heat, uncovered, for 2 hours or until the beans are tender. Remove the soup pot from the heat, and discard the bay leaf and thyme.

Rub the beans through a sieve or purée them in a blender or food processor, and strain. Add the sherry and salt and pepper to taste. (The salt pork will render some salt.)

Garnish each bowl of soup with a sprinkling of chopped egg and parsley. Slice the salt pork thinly, and serve it in the soup or as a side dish.

Serves 6.

One of the dining rooms at Maison Pierre.

Tournedos Andalouse

¼ cup olive oil
3 chopped garlic cloves
2 medium onions, chopped
2 medium bell peppers, chopped
1 large eggplant, diced into bite-size
  pieces
1 cup white wine

2 cups peeled, chopped tomatoes
salt to taste
pepper to taste
12 3½-oz. tournedos of beef, brushed
  with butter and broiled to individual
  taste
chopped parsley, for garnish

To make the Andalouse sauce, heat the olive oil in a skillet over medium heat, and lightly brown the garlic. Add the onions and bell peppers, and sauté the mixture for approximately 10 minutes. Add the eggplant and white wine, and simmer the sauce, stirring occasionally, for 10–15 minutes. Stir in tomatoes and salt and pepper to taste.

Spoon the Andalouse sauce onto six heated serving plates. Top each plate with two tournedos. Garnish each plate with a sprinkling of chopped parsley, and serve.

Serves 6.

Café Pierre

6 tsp. Mandarine Napoléon Liqueur
6 jiggers of amaretto

1 pot chickory coffee
whipped cream

Fill each of six cups with chickory coffee to about ½ inch from the top. Add 1 teaspoon of Mandarine Napoléon Liqueur to each cup. Add a full jigger of amaretto to each cup. Top each cup with whipped cream.

Serves 6.

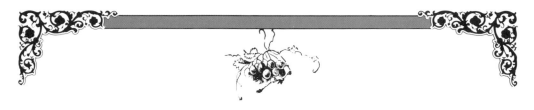

MANALE'S

1838 Napoleon Avenue

In 1913 Frank Manale started a small neighborhood Italian–New Orleans-style restaurant on Napoleon Avenue. Today, with the fourth generation assisting in the operation, Pascal's Manale Restaurant is one of the most popular dining spots among locals.

Frank's nephews aided in the operation until his death in the late 1940s. His nephew Pascal then bought the business. Pascal's daughter Frances Redosta Difelice and her husband Steve now own the restaurant.

The bar in Manale's, with its picture-lined walls and clubby atmosphere, offers some of the finest freshly shucked oysters in New Orleans. Waiting for a table is a pleasant part of the Manale's dining experience.

Exterior of Manale's.

Combination Pan Roast

1½ cups oyster water (the oyster liquor
  plus water to measure 1½ cups)
3 doz. fresh shucked oysters (reserve the
  liquor)
1½ cups milk
2 sticks butter or margarine
¾ cup flour
1½ cups chopped green onions (with
  tops)

½ cup chopped white onion
½ cup chopped parsley
1½ tbs. Worcestershire sauce
¾ tsp. Tabasco
¾ tsp. salt
¾ lb. lump crabmeat
½ cup bread crumbs

Bring the oyster water to a boil, add the oysters, and continue to boil until the edges
of the oysters curl (about 2 minutes). Strain the oysters from the water, and set them
aside. Add the milk to the oyster water, and let the mixture come to a boil. Turn off
the heat.

Melt the butter in a large skillet and stir in the flour. Cook the roux over low heat for
5 minutes, stirring occasionally. Add the green onions, white onions, and parsley,
and cook 5 minutes longer. Pour the hot milk and oyster water into the skillet, stirring until the mixture is well blended. Add the Worcestershire sauce, Tabasco, and
salt. Fold in the crabmeat, and cook the mixture over low heat for 20 minutes.

In each of six individual casseroles or ramekins layer 6 oysters, ⅔ cup of the crabmeat mixture, and 1 heaping tablespoon of bread crumbs. Place the casseroles or
ramekins under the broiler until they are browned, and serve.

Serves 6.

Pascal's Supreme Salad

House Dressing:
    1 cup plus 2 tbs. olive oil
    1/2 cup red wine vinegar
    1 1/2 tbs. Creole mustard
    1 tsp. orégano leaves
    1/2 tsp. Tabasco
    1/2 tsp. freshly ground black pepper
    1 tsp. salt
    1/4 tsp. finely chopped garlic
Rémoulade:
    1 tbs. dry mustard
    1 egg
    1 tsp. salt
    1 tbs. lemon juice
    1 cup oil
    1 tsp. water
    1 tbs. finely chopped green onion

3 tbs. finely chopped celery
1 tbs. finely chopped green olives
1 tbs. finely chopped dill pickle
1/2 hard-boiled egg, finely chopped
1 tbs. Creole mustard
1 tsp. Worcestershire sauce
1 tsp. A.1. sauce
6 lettuce leaves
1 1/2 cups diced celery
1 1/2 cups sliced bell peppers
18 thin slices onion
6 small tomatoes, quartered
18 black olives
18 anchovy fillets
6 artichoke hearts, quartered

To make the house dressing, combine all the ingredients well.

To make the rémoulade, mix the first four ingredients in a blender. Add the oil in a thin stream with the blender on high speed. This will produce a thick, creamy mayonnaise. Thin the mayonnaise with the water. Stir the green onion, celery, olives, dill pickle, hard-boiled egg, mustard, Worcestershire sauce, and A.1. sauce into the mayonnaise until well combined.

Line each of six salad plates with a lettuce leaf. Divide the remaining ingredients equally, and arrange them in an attractive manner on each plate. Serve each salad with 2 tablespoons of the house dressing and 2 tablespoons of the rémoulade.

Serves 6.

Shrimp a la Scarpia

1 stick butter
1½ lbs. small peeled shrimp
½ cup olive oil
4 tbs. chopped garlic
1 lb. spaghettini

2 tbs. chopped parsley
salt to taste
freshly ground black pepper to taste
grated Parmesan cheese to taste

Melt the butter in a skillet, and add the shrimp. Sauté the shrimp over medium heat for 10 minutes. Add the olive oil and garlic, and sauté the mixture 5 minutes more. Reduce the heat to low, and simmer the shrimp for 10 minutes.

Prepare the spaghettini according to package directions.

Stir the parsley into the shrimp before serving.

Allow ½ cup shrimp with sauce and equal portions of cooked spaghettini per serving. Add salt, freshly ground black pepper, and grated Parmesan cheese.

Serves 6.

Italian Cream Pecan Cake

Batter:
    1 cup shortening, room temperature
    1 cup sugar
    5 eggs
    2 cups flour
    1 tsp. baking soda
    pinch of salt
    1 cup buttermilk
    1 tsp. vanilla

    1 cup chopped pecans
    1 cup shredded coconut
Icing:
    2 sticks butter or margarine, room
      temperature
    8 oz. cream cheese, room temperature
    1 tsp. vanilla
    1 lb. powdered sugar
    1 cup chopped pecans

Preheat the oven to 350 degrees.

To prepare the batter, cream the shortening and sugar with an electric mixer. Add the eggs, one at a time, thoroughly mixing after each addition. Mix the flour, baking soda, and salt together in a separate bowl. Add a portion of the dry ingredients to the creamed mixture, and blend thoroughly. Add part of the buttermilk, and again blend completely. Repeat this procedure several times, ending with the flour mixture. Add 1 teaspoon of vanilla, and mix thoroughly. Fold in 1 cup of pecans and the coconut.

Pour the batter into three 8-inch square or round greased and floured baking pans. Bake the layers in the oven for 20–25 minutes or until a toothpick inserted in the center of the layers comes out clean. Remove the layers from the oven, cool them slightly, then turn them onto racks to cool completely before icing.

To prepare the icing, cream the butter or margarine, cream cheese, and 1 teaspoon of vanilla with an electric mixer. Gradually add the powdered sugar until thoroughly mixed. Fold in 1 cup of pecans. Ice the cake when the layers are completely cooled.

Serves 8.

Clockwise from top: Pascal's Supreme Salad, slice of Italian Cream Pecan Cake, Shrimp a la Scarpia, Combination Pan Roast, Italian Cream Pecan Cake.

MARTI'S

1041 Dumaine Street

After studying architecture at LSU, city planning at Columbia, fine arts at New York University, and apprenticing as an architect, Marti Shambra opened a restaurant.

Feeling that New Orleans patrons needed "home-cooked" Creole dishes served in a restaurant, Marti found a location on Rampart Street at Dumaine that was previously the Gentillich Grocery and Restaurant. With his family chef Henry J. Robinson, Marti has presented authentic Creole cooking in an atmosphere of New Orleans' past. The restaurant boasts an antique bar and Bellocq prints, and a traditional red dining room with tiled floors and brass chandeliers.

Oysters Marti

3 sticks butter
2¼ cups (about 3 bunches) chopped green
    onions (use white and green parts)
6 doz. small- to medium-size oysters,
    drained
1 tbs. finely chopped garlic

6 bay leaves
⅛ tsp. thyme
½ tsp. black pepper
½ cup flour
¼–½ tsp. salt (depending on the saltiness
    of the oysters)

Melt the butter in a skillet, and sauté the green onions until they are transparent (about 3 minutes). Add the oysters, garlic, bay leaves, thyme, and black pepper. Sift the flour over this mixture, and continue to sauté for 5 minutes or until the oysters are firm. Add salt to taste.

Serve in 6 ramekins with French bread on the side.

Serves 6 as an appetizer.

Crawfish Curry Soup

2 tbs. vegetable oil
2 tbs. butter
4 tbs. flour
1 cup finely chopped celery
½ cup finely chopped onions
3 tbs. finely chopped green onions (white and green parts)
1 tsp. minced garlic
¼ lb. crawfish fat (if available)
10 cups shrimp stock
2 bay leaves

⅛ tsp. powdered thyme
¼ cup tomato paste
½ cup peeled, seeded, and finely chopped tomato
½ lb. boiled and peeled crawfish (¼ lb. chopped, ¼ lb. whole)
2 tsp. or more curry powder, or to taste
salt to taste
½ tsp. cayenne
½ tsp. pepper

Heat the oil and butter in a skillet. Add the flour, and cook the roux over medium-low heat, stirring constantly, until it turns nut brown (approximately 10–15 minutes). Add the celery, onions, green onions, and garlic, and cook the vegetables until they are tender. Stir constantly. Turn down the heat if the vegetables begin to stick. Blend in the crawfish fat. Add the stock, bay leaves, thyme, tomato paste, tomato, and chopped crawfish. Simmer the soup for 45 minutes. Skim the top. Add the curry and remaining crawfish meat. Season the soup with salt, cayenne, and pepper. Cook the soup until the crawfish are well heated.

Serves 6.

Marti's.

Clockwise from top right: Oysters en Brochette, Peach Bread Pudding, Stuffed Eggplant, Crawfish Curry Soup.

Stuffed Eggplant

3 medium eggplants
¼ lb. (1 stick) butter
1 medium onion, finely chopped
¼ cup finely chopped green onions (white and green parts)
¼ cup finely chopped bell pepper
½ cup finely chopped celery
¼ tbs. chopped garlic
¼ cup finely chopped parsley
2 bay leaves
½ tbs. thyme leaves
1 lb. lump crabmeat
1¼ lbs. boiled medium-small shrimp

¼ lb. bacon, diced
6 tbs. reserved bacon grease (or add enough oil to the bacon grease to make up 6 tbs.)
1 tsp. salt
¾ tsp. black pepper
1 egg, beaten
1 cup bread crumbs (reserve ¼ cup for topping)
1 tbs. Parmesan cheese
¼ tsp. paprika
¼ cup (½ stick) melted butter

Cut the eggplants in half lengthwise. Place in a pot, cover with water, and bring to a boil. Boil for 15–20 minutes until tender. Pour off the water, and place the eggplants in a colander. Rinse with cold water. Place the eggplants cut side down in the colander, and allow them to drain until they are cool. Remove the meat from the eggplants, leaving a shell about ¼ inch thick. Finely chop the meat.

In a large saucepan melt 1 stick of butter. Add the onion, green onions, bell pepper, celery, garlic, parsley, and eggplant meat. Add the bay leaves and thyme. Sauté the mixture for 15 minutes until it is tender. Add the crabmeat and shrimp, and sauté the mixture for 5 minutes more and set it aside.

In a frying pan cook the diced bacon until it is crisp. Add the bacon and 6 tablespoons of drippings to the eggplant mixture, and sauté the stuffing for 10 minutes. Remove the bay leaves. Add salt and pepper to the stuffing, and mix well. Remove the stuffing from the heat, and let it stand for 5 minutes to cool. Add the beaten egg, and mix well. Add ¾ cup of the bread crumbs, and again mix well.

Fill the eggplant shells with the stuffing, and top with a mixture of the remaining ¼ cup bread crumbs, Parmesan cheese, and paprika. Drizzle the tops of the stuffed eggplants with melted butter, and bake in a 375-degree oven for 20 minutes.

Serves 6.

Peach Bread Pudding
with Spice Sauce

1 8-oz. loaf stale French bread
5 eggs, lightly beaten
½ cup sugar
¼ tbs. nutmeg
¼ tbs. cinnamon
2 tbs. vanilla

2 drops yellow food coloring
dash of salt
2 cups milk
½ cup canned peaches, drained and
  chopped (if using fresh peaches, peel)
6 tbs. melted butter

Preheat the oven to 350 degrees.

Dice the French bread, and set it aside.

Combine the remaining ingredients in a large mixing bowl, and blend well. Fold in the bread, and allow it to absorb the flavors.

Turn the pudding into a greased 9 inch by 12 inch pan. Set this pan into a larger pan of water. The water should come halfway up the sides of the bread-pudding pan. Bake the pudding uncovered in the oven for about 1 hour 20 minutes, or until the top of the pudding is lightly browned and a knife inserted in the middle of it comes out clean. Serve the pudding hot with Marti's Spice Sauce (see recipe, below).

Serves 8.

Marti's Spice Sauce

1 stick butter
¼ cup flour
2 cups milk
¾ cup sugar

½ tbs. nutmeg
½ tbs. cinnamon
2 drops yellow food coloring
1½ tbs. brandy

In a heavy saucepan melt the butter over medium heat, and add the flour, stirring the roux until the flour is cooked (at least 5 minutes). Gradually blend in the milk. Then add the sugar, spices, and food coloring. Stir until the sauce thickens. When the sauce has thickened, blend in the brandy and serve the sauce over bread pudding.

Yield: 2¾ cups.

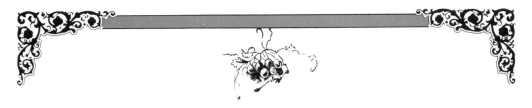

MASSON'S BEACH HOUSE

7200 Pontchartrain Boulevard

In 1915 Albert Dubos and his wife opened the Bungalow near the shore of Lake Pontchartrain. For twenty-five years they entertained at their table the epicures of New Orleans. Their daughter, after having grown up in the restaurant, studied the culinary arts in France. When her husband Ernest Masson retired as a pharmacist, the Bungalow reopened as Masson's under their proprietorship. The Masson children, Ernest Jr. and Albert, were sent to France upon completion of their military service—Ernest to learn cuisine and Albert to learn wines. Through the years, both have received numerous awards and testimonials for their knowledge.

Albert now directs the operation. He is assisted by his cousin, Executive Chef Robert Finley, who has been at Masson's since 1955, and Vincent Liberto, who joined the restaurant in 1959 and is now general manager.

Exterior of Masson's.

Crabmeat and Artichoke

6 fresh artichokes
¾ stick (6 tbs.) butter or margarine
⅔ cup thinly sliced green onions
pinch (¹⁄₁₆ tsp.) thyme leaves
2 bay leaves
pinch cayenne
½ tsp. salt
¼ cup white wine
1 lb. lump crabmeat

1 egg, beaten
½ cup bread crumbs
½ cup finely grated Swiss cheese
Hollandaise Sauce:
   3 egg yolks
   2 tbs. lemon juice
   ¼ tsp. salt
   pinch of cayenne
   1 stick butter

In a large soup pot boil the artichokes in salted water to cover for 30–40 minutes or until the leaves can be easily pulled from the base. Drain the artichokes, and set them aside to cool. Remove the leaves and the "hair" from the base of the artichokes, and reserve the bottoms for the recipe. (The leaves may be used in other recipes.)

Preheat the oven to 350 degrees.

Melt ¾ stick of butter or margarine in a skillet, and sauté the green onions, thyme, bay leaves, and cayenne over medium-high heat for 3 minutes. Add the salt, wine, and crabmeat, and stir the mixture until the crabmeat is heated. Remove the mixture from the heat, and mix the egg and bread crumbs into it.

Using ½ cup of crabmeat mixture per serving, form it into six balls, and place each ball on top of an artichoke bottom. Sprinkle with a heaping tablespoon of grated Swiss cheese. Bake the artichoke bottoms for 15 minutes.

Make the hollandaise. Place the egg yolks, lemon juice, salt, and cayenne in a blender, and blend for a few seconds on medium speed.

In a small saucepan, bring 1 stick of butter to a boil but do not brown. With the blender on high speed, add the hot butter in a slow, steady stream until the sauce is well blended.

Top each baked crabmeat and artichoke with 2 heaping tablespoons of hollandaise, and serve.

Serves 6.

Turtle Soup

3 veal tails, cut in 2-inch pieces
1 gallon water
4 bay leaves
4 whole cloves
4 whole allspice
½ tsp. thyme
peelings and trimmings from soup
   vegetables (below)
1½ lbs. diced turtle meat
6 tbs. butter or margarine
2 cups chopped onions
1 cup chopped celery tops
1 cup chopped bell peppers

1 cup chopped carrots
½ tbs. chopped garlic
½ cup flour
1 6-oz. can tomato paste
¼ tsp. cayenne
1 tsp. salt
juice of 1 lemon
2 cups dry sherry
2 hard-boiled eggs, chopped
¼ cup chopped parsley
lemon slices, for garnish
parsley, for garnish

In a large pot simmer the veal tails in the water for 1 hour, skimming often. Add the bay leaves, cloves, allspice, thyme, and vegetable peelings and trimmings, and simmer for 2 more hours. Strain the stock, and set aside.

In a clean soup pot, brown the turtle meat in the butter or margarine. Add the onions, celery tops, bell peppers, carrots, and garlic, and sauté the vegetables until they are soft, about 20 minutes. Stir in the flour, and cook the mixture 10 minutes more. Add the strained stock, tomato paste, cayenne, and salt. Simmer the soup for 1½ hours. Turn off the heat, and stir in the lemon juice, sherry, chopped eggs, and parsley.

Garnish each serving with a slice of lemon and a sprinkling of chopped parsley.

Serves 6–8.

Potatoes Masson

¾ lb. peeled potatoes, thinly sliced
1½ cups light cream
3 eggs, beaten

¾ tsp. salt
½ tsp. freshly ground black pepper
¼ cup grated cheddar cheese

Preheat the oven to 350 degrees.

Lay the sliced potatoes in a buttered casserole. Combine the cream, eggs, salt, and pepper. Pour the mixture over the potatoes. Top the dish with the grated cheese.

Bake uncovered in the oven for 30 minutes or until a knife inserted in the center of the potatoes comes out clean.

Serves 4.

Poisson du Bayou Dubos

Oyster Dressing:
    3 tbs. finely chopped green onions (green
      and white parts)
    1/16 tsp. ground thyme
    1/16 tsp. cayenne
    1/16 tsp. garlic powder
    1½ tbs. butter
    1 cup drained, chopped oysters
    ¼–½ cup bread crumbs
    ¼ tsp. salt or, if using salty oysters, salt
      to taste
6 8-oz. trout fillets
Béarnaise:
    4 egg yolks

1 tbs. lemon juice
3 tbs. tarragon vinegar
½ tsp. salt
⅛ tsp. cayenne
2 sticks melted butter, warmed
2 tbs. minced onion
1 tbs. minced tarragon leaves (pickled or
    dried)
1 tbs. chopped parsley
3 doz. crab claws
3 lemons, halved, and tied in gauze

To make the oyster dressing, lightly sauté the green onions, thyme, cayenne, and garlic powder in the butter. Add the chopped oysters, and simmer for 5 minutes. Add enough of the bread crumbs to absorb all of the oyster juice. Add salt to taste.

Clockwise from top: Crabmeat Canapé, Turtle Soup, Poisson du Bayou Dubos, Potatoes Masson, Sabayon.

Roll each trout fillet around two or three fingers, and pin each together with a tooth-pick. Place the fillets upright in a small greased baking pan. Fill the fillets with the oyster dressing, and bake them for 20–30 minutes (depending on the thickness of the fillets) in a 350-degree oven until they are flaky.

To make the Béarnaise, beat the egg yolks together with the lemon juice, 1 table-spoon of tarragon vinegar, salt, and cayenne, and pour the mixture in the top of a double boiler. Cook the mixture over low heat, whisking constantly, being careful never to let the water in the double boiler come to a boil. Continue cooking the mix-ture until it thickens slightly and becomes completely foamy. Beat in the warm butter a little at a time. Cook the sauce until it has thickened. Remove the sauce from heat if it gets too hot.

In another saucepan, add the onion, tarragon leaves, and 2 tablespoons of tarragon vinegar. Cook the mixture until the liquid is completely reduced. Cool the mixture slightly, and blend it into the thickened sauce. Add the parsley.

Lightly steam the crab claws until they are hot.

Set each fish fillet on a plate, and cover it with Béarnaise (about ¼ cup per serving). Garnish each dish with crab claws and half a lemon.

Serves 6.

Sabayon

6 eggs, separated and at room
  temperature
¾ cup sugar
¾ cup cream sherry

¾ cup heavy cream, chilled
1 tsp. vanilla
¼ tsp. cream of tartar

In the top of a double boiler whisk the 6 egg yolks and sugar. Add the sherry, and cook the mixture until it is thickened, about 15 minutes. Pour the mixture into a bowl, and cool it for about 15 minutes.

Meanwhile, whip the cream until it forms peaks. Stir the vanilla into the whipped cream, and fold the cream into the cooled egg-yolk mixture.

In a clean mixing bowl, beat the egg whites with the cream of tartar until stiff peaks form. Fold the egg whites into the other mixture.

Divide the sabayon among six individual ramekins, and refrigerate it for 2–3 hours before serving.

Serves 6.

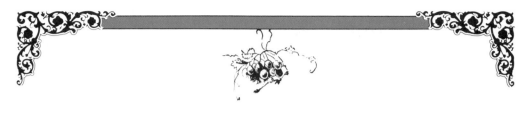

MAYLIE'S

1009 Poydras Street

Maylie's is one of the true Creole restaurants in New Orleans. Bernard Maylie and Hypolite Esparbe co-owned a coffee stall in the market. Their flourishing business enabled them to move to a café on the corner of Poydras and Dryades Streets, and in 1876 La Maison Maylie et Esparbe was opened.

In the tradition of Madame Begue, Maylie and Esparbe and their French wives, who were sisters, served an eleven-o'clock breakfast to their patrons, workers in the market. The wives, daughters of an innkeeper, had had experience in the kitchen and the dining room.

In 1903 William Maylie joined his father and uncle in the business. By 1912 both Maylie and Esparbe had died. Their wives carried on, with Willie doing the buying and his brother John overseeing the dining room.

In 1939 the third generation stepped in. William L. Maylie, grandson of the founder, started work at the restaurant. In 1946 he bought the restaurant, and his wife Anna May Deano Maylie began assisting him in the day-to-day operation of the establishment. And now a fourth generation waits in the wings.

Clockwise from top: Baked Brussels Sprouts au Gratin, Liquored Cracklin' Bread, Deviled Eggs with Rémoulade Sauce, Daube Glacé, Whiskey Prune Pie.

145

Deviled Eggs with Rémoulade Sauce

1 doz. hard-boiled eggs
½ tbs. salt
3 tbs. mayonnaise
½ cup sweet relish
Rémoulade Sauce:
   1 cup Creole mustard
   6 tbs. olive oil
   3 tbs. ketchup

1 tbs. vinegar
1 tbs. lemon juice
2 tbs. finely chopped green onions
½ cup minced celery heart (plus leaves)
salt to taste
pepper to taste
6 lettuce leaves

Place the eggs in a pot with cool water to cover and the salt. Bring the water to a boil, and continue to boil for 10 minutes. Remove the eggs from the heat, pour off the water, and cool the eggs by immersing them in cold water.

Peel and halve the eggs. Remove the yolks from eggs, and mash the yolks in a mixing bowl with a fork. Add the mayonnaise and relish, and mix well.

Fill the egg whites with the egg-yolk mixture, and refrigerate the eggs before serving them.

To make the rémoulade sauce, combine all the ingredients. This keeps well in the refrigerator.

Line each of six salad plates with a lettuce leaf, and place 4 egg halves on each plate. Top each egg half with a tablespoon of rémoulade sauce.

Serves 6.

Daube Glacé

1 thick round of beef, with bone, about
   3 lbs. (Have the butcher lard the meat
   with diced squares of fresh pork fat.)
2 cups claret
8 green onions, coarsely chopped (white
   and green parts)
2 ribs celery, coarsely chopped
2 carrots, cut into large pieces
1 green pepper, sliced
1 tbs. chopped parsley
3 cloves garlic

¼ tsp. dried thyme leaves or 1 large
   sprig fresh thyme
4 peppercorns
1 bay leaf
1 tbs. salt
22 cups cold water
2 pig's feet
2 calf's feet
lemon slices, for garnish
minced parsley, for garnish

Soak the round of beef overnight in the refrigerator with the claret, green onions, celery, carrots, green pepper, parsley, garlic, thyme, peppercorns, bay leaf, and salt.

In the morning, put the above ingredients in a soup pot, and cover them with the cold water. Add the pig's feet and calf's feet, and let the mixture come to a boil. Reduce the heat, cover, and simmer the mixture for approximately 4 hours until you can remove the bones from the meat and feet. In the course of simmering, remove the fat that will rise to the top of the liquid. Since the carrots will be cooked before the meat, remove them when they are done and slice them, arranging them in the bottom of a medium-size mold. Just before the meat and feet are ready, taste for salt and black pepper. More may be needed.

When the meat and feet are ready, turn off the heat. When cool enough to handle, remove the meat and feet from the liquid, remove the bones, and place pieces of meat in the bottom of the mold on top of the carrots.

Strain the liquid, and skim most of the fat from the top. Pour the liquid into the mold over the meat.

To garnish, place lemon slices and parsley on top of the mold.

Place the mold in the refrigerator to congeal.

Unmold the Daube Glacé, and slice.

Serves 6–8.

Liquored Cracklin' Bread

¾ cup corn flour
¾ cup yellow cornmeal
1½ tsp. baking powder
½ tsp. salt
1 cup water
1 bay leaf

½ tbs. lard or shortening
½ cup milk
2 tbs. Pernod or Herbsaint
¾ cup broken cracklin's
shortening for deep frying
sifted powdered sugar

Sift the corn flour, cornmeal, baking powder, and salt into a mixing bowl.

Bring the water with the bay leaf to a boil. Remove the water from the heat, and discard the bay leaf.

Pour the water over the dry ingredients. Add the lard or shortening, and stir the mixture until it is well combined. Stir in the milk and Pernod or Herbsaint. Fold in the broken cracklin's.

Heat the shortening in a deep fryer, and drop in the mixture by the heaping tablespoonful, hush-puppy style. Fry the breads until they are golden brown. Drain them on paper towels.

Sprinkle the cracklin' breads with powdered sugar, and serve them hot.

Serves 6.

Baked Brussels Sprouts au Gratin

1 quart fresh Brussels sprouts
2 tbs. butter
½ cup chopped green onions
1 tbs. flour
½ slice bacon
½ tbs. chopped garlic
½ tbs. chopped parsley

1 cup water, reserved from boiling the
   Brussels sprouts
½ tsp. salt
⅛ tsp. pepper
½ cup grated cheddar cheese
2½ tbs. bread crumbs

Preheat the oven to 325 degrees.

Wash the Brussels sprouts, and remove any discolored outer leaves. With a small paring knife, make a cross-shaped incision ¼ inch deep in the base of each sprout to allow even cooking. Bring a pot of water to a boil (enough to cover the sprouts). Add the sprouts, let the water return to a boil, and simmer the sprouts for approximately 10 minutes or until the sprouts are tender. Drain and reserve 1 cup of hot liquid.

Melt the butter in a small skillet. Add the green onions, and sauté them for 3 minutes. Stir in the flour, and cook the mixture until the flour is dissolved (about 3 minutes). Add the bacon, garlic, and parsley, and cook the mixture 3 more minutes. Pour in the reserved Brussels sprouts water, add salt and pepper, and bring the mixture to a boil, stirring constantly until it is thickened to the consistency of heavy cream. Remove the bacon from the sauce.

Place the Brussels sprouts base down in a buttered casserole or baking pan. Pour the sauce over the sprouts. Top the sprouts first with grated cheese and then with bread crumbs.

Bake the sprouts in the oven for 30 minutes or until the top is browned.

Serves 6.

Whiskey Prune Pie

1 lb. dried extra-large prunes (preferably
   pitted)
¼ lemon
¾ cup sugar
⅓ cup whiskey
½ cup chopped pecans

Pie Crust:
   ⅔ cup chilled shortening
   2 tbs. chilled butter
   2 cups flour, sifted
   ½ tsp. salt
   4 tbs. cold water
   melted butter
powdered sugar

Soak the prunes overnight in water to cover.

Pour the prunes and the water into a saucepan, adding more water, if needed, to cover. Over high heat, bring the prunes with the lemon and sugar to a boil. Reduce the heat to low, and cook the prunes for approximately 20–25 minutes until the liquid is syrupy. Remove the lemon. Cool and reserve the syrup, pit the prunes (if pitted prunes are unavailable), and add the whiskey.

Preheat the oven to 400 degrees.

To prepare the pie crust, cut the shortening and butter into the flour and salt. When the shortening and butter are broken into pea-size pieces, slowly add enough water to form a ball. Divide the dough ball into two equal parts. Place them in the freezer for 10 minutes before rolling out the bottom crust between two sheets of floured waxed paper. Fit the bottom crust into a 9-inch or 10-inch pie plate, and brush it with melted butter. Pour in the pie filling. Roll out the top crust, and cut it into ½-inch strips to form a lattice. Trim the crust.

Bake the pie in the oven for 10 minutes. Reduce the heat to 325 degrees, and bake the pie for approximately 40 minutes more or until it turns golden brown.

When the pie is cool, sprinkle it with powdered sugar.

Serves 6.

MR. B'S BISTRO
201 Royal Street

Mr. B's is the new child of the Brennans—Ella, Adelaide, John, and Dick. Wanting to create a restaurant that was not expensive yet with good quality food and an attractive atmosphere, they developed Mr. B's Bistro. Located on Royal Street where Solari's was, the Brennans have brought to the French Quarter a new restaurant with a fresh menu.

The home-made pastas, the hickory-grilled meats and fish, the coconut-batter shrimp, and the high-quality "American only" wine list are all typical touches of the Brennan drive for individuality. Mr. B's is a pleasant, relatively informal bistro, where one can relax, dine well, and enjoy the parade on the Rue Royal.

Baked Brie

6 4½-oz. Brie rounds
6 tsp. butter
6 tbs. lightly toasted sliced almonds

Delicious apple slices, strawberries, or
   grapes, for garnish

Top each Brie round with 1 teaspoon of butter and 1 tablespoon of almonds.

Bake the Brie in individual ramekins in a 400-degree oven for 4 minutes or until the cheese is crusty on the outside and runny on the inside.

Garnish each serving with Delicious apple slices, strawberries, or grapes.

Serve with hot French bread.

Serves 6.

Shrimp Chippewa

5 doz. fresh medium-sized raw shrimp
18 oz. fresh mushrooms
Velouté Sauce:
    9 tbs. butter
    9 tbs. flour
    4½ cups fish stock
    dash nutmeg
    white pepper to taste
    salt to taste
    1 tsp. butter
6 tbs. finely chopped green onions (white
    and green parts)

1½ cups fish stock
1 tbs. finely chopped garlic
1 tsp. garlic powder
1 tsp. onion powder
1 tsp. black pepper
1 tsp. cayenne
½ tsp. salt
½ tsp. orégano
½ tsp. powdered thyme
½ tsp. paprika
6 2-inch slices French bread

Butterfly the shrimp, and remove the head and peel all but the final tail segment. Cut lengthwise down the underside of the shrimp, but do not cut completely through. Devein the shrimp. Set them aside.

Wash and trim the mushrooms, and cut them into quarters. Set them aside.

To make the velouté sauce, melt 9 tablespoons of butter in a heavy saucepan. Stir in the flour, and cook the roux for 3–5 minutes over medium heat until the flour is dissolved. Stir in 4½ cups of fish stock gradually to avoid lumps. Continue to cook the sauce for approximately 20 minutes, allowing the sauce to come to a boil and then reducing the heat and simmering it gently until it reaches the consistency of a cream sauce. Remove the sauce from the heat, and season it to taste with nutmeg, pepper, and salt. Melt a pat of butter on the top of the sauce to prevent a skin from forming. Set the sauce aside.

In a large skillet poach the shrimp, mushrooms, and green onions in 1½ cups of fish stock over medium-high heat for 5–8 minutes. Season the mixture with the garlic, garlic powder, onion powder, pepper, cayenne, salt, orégano, thyme, and paprika. Blend in the velouté sauce, and heat gently.

Serve the shrimp in individual bowls with sliced French bread on the side.

Serves 6.

Crabmeat Salad

6 Boston lettuce leaves
3 cups Boston-romaine lettuce mixture,
   shredded
1 lb. backfin lump crabmeat
3 hard-boiled eggs, quartered
6 tomato wedges
⅔ cup sliced zucchini and yellow-squash
   mixture, marinated in oil and vinegar to
   cover

Louis Dressing:
   1 cup mayonnaise
   ¼ cup ketchup
   ¼ cup chili sauce
   2 tbs. finely chopped green onions (white
      and green parts)
   ⅛ tsp. horseradish
   1½ tsp. olive oil
   salt to taste
   pepper to taste

Line the plates with the Boston lettuce leaves, and divide the shredded lettuce on top. Place the crabmeat over the shredded lettuce, and garnish with the eggs, tomato wedges, and zucchini and squash mixture.

Mix the ingredients for the Louis dressing, and serve it on the side.

Serves 6 as a salad or 3 as an entrée.

Preparation of crabmeat salad by Amy Texido, with Chef Jimmy Smith in background.

Clockwise from right: Amaretto Cream, Shrimp Chippewa, Baked Brie, Crabmeat Salad.

154

Amaretto Cream

3 egg yolks
⅓ cup sugar
2 tbs. flour
1 cup milk
½ tbs. vanilla

½ cup amaretto
2 cups heavy cream, cold
½ cup sifted powdered sugar
6 fresh strawberries, for garnish

In a mixing bowl, whisk together the egg yolks, sugar, and flour until the mixture is light and creamy.

Scald the milk in a saucepan, and pour it into the egg-yolk mixture, whisking constantly to prevent the egg yolks from cooking. Continue to whisk until the mixture is foamy. Cook the mixture slowly over medium heat for about 10 minutes or until it has thickened to a custardlike consistency. Once this mixture has thickened, place the saucepan in a bowl of ice and whisk the mixture constantly until it has cooled completely. Stir in the vanilla and amaretto.

Whip the cold cream in a mixing bowl until it forms soft peaks. Add the powdered sugar, and continue to whip until the cream forms stiff peaks.

Pour the custard mixture into the whipped cream, and gently fold it in until it is well combined. Spoon the custard into six 1-cup dessert glasses, and garnish each serving with a strawberry. Chill the desserts for several hours before serving.

Serves 6.

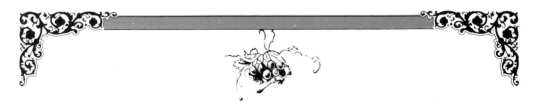

MORAN'S RIVERSIDE

French Market Complex

Jimmy Moran of Moran's Riverside grew up in his mother's kitchen in the French Quarter. His father, "Diamond" Jim Moran, was the owner and operator of a famous restaurant, La Louisiane. Mrs. Moran cooked the restaurant's dishes in her home, and they were transported to the establishment. Since he had been around the restaurant business and wonderful food all his life, when Jimmy entered the service, he was a chef to many top officers.

After graduating from LSU, Jimmy was approached by several airlines to create special dishes for their international flights to Venezuela, Cuba, and other destinations. With Delta, Braniff, and Eastern now clients, this opportunity became so lucrative that Jimmy constructed the first all-electric kitchen in New Orleans (located near the Moissant Airport).

During the eight years in which the airlines catering business was booming, Jimmy opened the Broadmoor Restaurant, now Jack Sabin's, in Baton Rouge. In 1950 he opened the Salt and Pepper Shop, which served hamburgers, and within that first year the demand for "good" hamburgers was so great that three more shops were opened.

In 1958 "Diamond Jim" passed away, and Jimmy took over the operation of La Louisiane. He soon leased the largest portion of the restaurant (which seated 700 people) to Playboy.

La Louisiane was operated by Jimmy until 1979, when he sold it to Joe Marcello, Jr. and Nick Mosca. Today Jimmy operates not only his Riverside restaurant but the Acme Oyster Bar and the Old Absinthe House.

Jimmy believes that the future of New Orleans is on the Mississippi River. Moran's Riverside is everything he has hoped, worked, and loved New Orleans for.

Fettuccini Alfredo

4 quarts water
¾ tsp. salt
1 lb. noodles (homemade, if available)
¼ lb. butter, room temperature

¼ lb. of Parmesan cheese, grated
¼ cup heavy cream, warmed
freshly ground pepper to taste

Place a 6-quart pot or larger with the water over high heat. Add the salt. Bring the water to a boil. When the water is boiling turbulently, add the noodles, separating them with a long-handled fork. Homemade noodles take one-quarter of the time to cook than store-bought noodles.

Place the pan or bowl you will mix the pasta in over the pot.

When the pasta is cooked to your liking, drain approximately 98 percent of the water.

Place the noodles in the preheated pan or bowl along with the butter. Stir gently until the butter is melted, adding half of the cheese and half of the cream. Continue to mix, and add the remainder of the cheese. If more moisture is needed, add the rest of the cream. Stir for a few seconds and serve, adding freshly ground pepper.

Serves 4.

Jimmy Moran preparing fettuccini.

Clockwise from center: Amaretto Parfait, Fettuccini Alfredo, Rack of Lamb, Crabmeat Dutch.

Crabmeat Dutch

6 Creole tomatoes, or regular tomatoes
6 fresh basil leaves, finely chopped
pinch of fresh thyme or ⅛ tsp. dried
   thyme leaves
2 tbs. grated Parmesan cheese
salt to taste

pepper to taste
2 lemons
1 lb. lump crabmeat, picked over
1 tbs. finely chopped parsley
6 parsley sprigs for garnish

Cut the tomatoes into medium-thick slices over a bowl. Add the basil, thyme, Parmesan, salt, and pepper. Mix gently so as not to break up the tomato slices. Squeeze the juice from one lemon into the bowl, and let this set for several minutes. Divide the other lemon into six wedges. Set the lemon wedges aside.

Divide the sliced tomatoes among six chilled plates, leaving the juice in the bowl. Add the crabmeat and parsley to the bowl, and mix them with the juices. Divide the crabmeat equally over the tomatoes, spooning over the juice.

Garnish each plate with a sprig of parsley and a wedge of lemon.

Serves 6.

Rack of Lamb

3 2½–3-lb. racks of lamb, chine bone
   removed

salt to taste
pepper to taste

The racks of lamb should be trimmed, but the layer of fat next to the meat should be left intact.

Rub the racks with salt and pepper.

Light a charcoal pit, using approximately 5 pounds of coal. Let the fire burn until the flames have died out and the coals glow.

Place the racks on a spit. Add to the pit pecan chips that have been soaked in water. If you have a cover, close the pit, leaving a small crack to allow the smoke to escape.

Cook and smoke the racks of lamb to taste.
   Rare: 20–25 minutes
   Medium: 25–30 minutes
   Well-done: over 35 minutes

Serves 6.

Amaretto Parfait

12 scoops French vanilla ice cream
6 oz. amaretto
6 tbs. toasted slivered almonds

½ cup heavy cream, whipped (no sugar
   added)
6 maraschino cherries

Place 2 scoops of ice cream in each of six dessert glasses, topping each glass with 2 tablespoons of amaretto. Sprinkle the almonds over the top, add the whipped cream, and serve with a cherry on top.

Serves 6.

MOSCA'S

Highway 90

The Mosca family had been in the restaurant business for two generations when they arrived in New Orleans in 1946 to open their new place. Given its beginnings as a roadhouse bar and dining room located across the Mississippi and a few miles down the road from the city, the probable success of the establishment should have been remote. But New Orleanians smelled the perfume of roasting garlic wafting across the river and instinctively beat a path to Mosca's door.

Nick and Johnny, Mary and her husband Vincent Marconi all helped Mama and Papa in the restaurant. As a family they cooked, served, cleaned, and attended to every duty. Mama Mosca did most of the cooking and supervised the others.

Papa Mosca died in 1962, leaving his able family to carry on. Nick Mosca branched out on his own and operated the Elmwood Plantation. He is now running La Louisiane. Mama died in 1979, leaving the restaurant to Johnny, Mary, and Vincent.

Through the years, little has changed at Mosca's. You'll find no elaborate décor or service here—only a simple roadhouse, a lovely family, and some of the best meals available.

Marinated Crab Salad

6 quarts water
4 tbs. salt
2 tsp. cayenne or 1 box crab boil
9 fresh crabs
2 cups olive oil, preferably Bertolli
1½ cups white vinegar

15 cloves unpeeled garlic, crushed
2 cups roughly chopped onions
1 tsp. salt
½ tsp. pepper
3 cups giardeniera (Italian pickled vege-
    table salad)

Bring the water, which has been seasoned with salt and cayenne or crab boil, to a boil. Add the crabs, and boil for 25 minutes. Remove the crabs from the water, and let them cool.

To prepare the crabs, discard the top shells and gills. Pull off the claws (but leave the legs on). Break the crab bodies in half. Set the crabs aside.

Mix the olive oil and vinegar in a large bowl.

Place the crab bodies and claws in the olive oil and vinegar mixture. Add the garlic, onions, salt, and pepper. Marinate the crabs in the refrigerator overnight.

To serve, put three crab halves and three crab claws on each of six plates. Top each serving with ½ cup of giardeniera and some of the marinade.

Serves 6.

Clockwise from right: Chicken a la Grande, Italian Shrimp, Marinated Crab Salad.

Italian Shrimp

2 lbs. large, whole fresh shrimp
1 cup olive oil
1 tbs. plus 1 tsp. salt
2 tsp. freshly ground black pepper
2 tsp. orégano leaves

2 tsp. rosemary leaves
3 bay leaves
25 cloves unpeeled garlic, mashed
1 cup dry white wine

Place all the ingredients except the wine in a large skillet, and cook over medium-high heat for 15–20 minutes or until the shrimp are pink and the liquid produced by the shrimp has almost completely disappeared. Stir occasionally. Reduce the heat, and add the wine. Cook at a low simmer until the liquid is reduced by half, about 5–7 minutes.

Serve the shrimp hot with the pan juices. French bread for dipping is a nice accompaniment.

Serves 6.

Chicken a la Grande

¾ cup Bertolli olive oil
2 3-lb. chickens, cut into eighths
½ tsp. salt
1 tsp. freshly ground black pepper

10 cloves unpeeled garlic, mashed
1 tsp. rosemary
1 tsp. orégano
1 cup dry white wine

In a large skillet, heat the olive oil until it is hot, and add the chicken pieces. Turn the chicken often, cooking the pieces until they are browned. Sprinkle the chicken pieces with salt and pepper. Add the garlic, rosemary, and orégano, stirring to distribute the seasonings. Pour the wine over the chicken, and simmer until the wine is reduced by half.

Serve the chicken hot with the pan juices.

Serves 6.

Cheesecake

Crust:
    1²/₃ cups graham-cracker crumbs
    ½ tsp. cinnamon
    3 tbs. sugar
    1 stick butter, melted

Filling:
    12 oz. Philadelphia-brand cream cheese,
      softened
    1 cup sour cream

½ cup sugar
3 eggs
1 tsp. grated lemon rind
1 tsp. strained lemon juice
1 tsp. vanilla

Icing:
    1 cup sour cream
    2 tbs. sugar
    ¼ tsp. vanilla

To make the crust, mix the graham-cracker crumbs, cinnamon, and 3 tablespoons of sugar together. Stir in the melted butter, and mix thoroughly. Press the mixture onto the bottom and sides of an 8-inch springform pan or an 8-inch square baking pan. Bake the crust at 375 degrees for 10 minutes, and cool it.

To make the filling, cream the cream cheese and 1 cup of sour cream with an electric mixer. Gradually add ½ cup of sugar. Mix in the eggs one at a time. Then add the lemon rind, lemon juice, and 1 teaspoon of vanilla, beating the mixture until it is fluffy. Pour the filling into the crust, and bake the cake at 350 degrees for 30 minutes. Turn off the oven, and let the cake sit in the oven for 30 minutes more.

Meanwhile, make the icing by whipping together 1 cup of sour cream, 2 tablespoons of sugar, and ¼ teaspoon of vanilla.

After the cheesecake has finished its second half hour of cooking, remove it from the oven, spread the icing on it, and return it to the oven for 10 minutes more.

The cheesecake may be served either warm or chilled.

Serves 8.

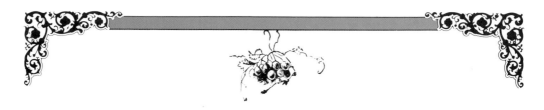

PARKER'S

365 Canal Street

Parker Barnes is a newcomer to New Orleans who has formulated a concept he knows will work. In the ten years he has spent in the business, he has worked in Waikiki, Denver, San Diego, Phoenix, Saratoga, Boston, Vermont, and Bar Harbor. A friend enticed him into a partnership in a restaurant located in the newly revitalized Quincy Market in Boston. Seeing the success of the entire Market Place project, Parker decided to venture out on his own. He went to friends at Chase Manhattan and Citibank in New York who had access to the bank computer system. They used the computer to determine which cities in the United States were going to undergo a downtown economic renovation within the next five years. The choices were New York, Seattle, and New Orleans. New Orleans intrigued him most.

Within a few weeks, Parker had put together financing and a loyal group of five key workers and came to New Orleans. For the next five months this ambitious group spread itself out and worked at different restaurants to get an understanding of New Orleans food and the attitudes of the people there.

Parker acquired the café St. Cecile in the French Market and reopened it as the Gazebo. He then realized that Canal Place would soon be available for occupancy and signed a lease there. So Parker's was born.

In the two years of Parker's existence the restaurant has given New Orleans a good, dependable menu with a unique but New Orleans flair. As the city grows at Canal and the Mississippi, so will Parker's.

Clockwise from top: Breads, Hot Duckling Salad, Crab Bisque, Shrimp Dijonnaise, Hot Duckling Salad, Baked Oysters Parker, Chocolate Mousse Pie.

Baked Oysters Parker

Rockefeller Sauce:

    1 1/2 cups oyster liquor (see below), well-reduced shrimp stock, or rich fish stock

    1 tsp. powdered fennel or crushed fennel seeds

    1 clove garlic, minced

    1/2 tsp. salt

    1 dash Worcestershire sauce

    1/4 tsp. white pepper

    2 tbs. Pernod or Herbsaint

    1 1/2 strips bacon, minced and cooked until crisp (reserve the grease)

    1/4 cup flour

    reserved bacon grease plus enough melted butter to make 1/4 cup

    1 10-oz. bag fresh spinach, washed, stemmed, and finely chopped

Mornay Sauce:

    1 cup milk

    1 cup whipping cream

    1/4 cup butter

    1/4 cup flour

    1/4 tsp. salt

    1/4 tsp. white pepper

    pinch nutmeg

    1/2 cup grated Gruyère cheese

36 freshly shucked oysters and their liquor

36 half oyster shells, well washed

3/4 cup bread crumbs

1 1/2 cups grated Gruyère cheese

2 lemons, quartered

6 sprigs parsley

To make the Rockefeller sauce, put the oyster liquor or stock, fennel, garlic, 1/2 teaspoon of salt, Worcestershire sauce, 1/4 teaspoon of pepper, Pernod or Herbsaint, and bacon in a saucepan. Bring the mixture to a boil. Set it aside.

In a saucepan, add enough melted butter to the reserved bacon grease to make 1/4 cup. Make a brown roux by cooking 1/4 cup of flour with the grease and butter, stirring constantly, until the roux has acquired a nut-brown color, about 10 minutes. Blend the roux into the saucepan with the other ingredients. Add the spinach, and mix thoroughly.

Cool before using.

To make the mornay sauce, bring the milk and cream to a boil in a saucepan. Set it aside.

In another saucepan, make a white roux by cooking 1/4 cup of butter with 1/4 cup of flour for 2–3 minutes, stirring constantly to prevent any browning. Blend the roux into the liquid. Add 1/4 teaspoon of salt, 1/4 teaspoon of white pepper, and the nutmeg. Stir in 1/2 cup of cheese, and continue heating until the cheese is completely melted.

Cool the sauce before using.

Preheat the oven to 350 degrees.

Place the oyster shells on baking pans. Place 1 teaspoon of Rockefeller sauce on the shell, top with an oyster, and top the oyster with 1 teaspoon of mornay sauce. Sprinkle with grated Gruyère and bread crumbs.

Bake the oysters in the oven for 20 minutes.

Serve six oysters per person, garnishing each platter with lemon wedges and parsley.

Serves 6.

Crab Bisque

5 cups shrimp stock or fish stock (Shrimp stock is made by boiling 1 lb. shrimp heads and shells in 3 quarts water for 35–40 minutes, then straining.)
½ cup butter
½ cup flour
1 cup whipping cream

⅔ cup sherry
⅛ tsp. cayenne
¼ tsp. white pepper
1 tsp. salt
½ lb. lump crabmeat
1 tbs. minced parsley

Bring the shrimp stock or fish stock to a boil.

Make a white roux by cooking the butter and flour together in a saucepan for 5 minutes, stirring to ensure consistent cooking. Do not allow the roux to brown. Mix the roux into the stock, and cook the mixture for 3 minutes until the bisque has thickened. Add the cream, sherry, cayenne, white pepper, and salt. Bring the bisque to a simmer, and cook it for a few minutes. Carefully fold in the crabmeat, and serve the bisque with a sprinkling of minced parsley on the top of each serving.

Serves 6.

Hot Duck Salad

1 4–5-lb. duck
salt
pepper
garlic powder
cayenne
cumin powder
Vinaigrette Dressing:
   1 tbs. Dijon mustard
   2 tbs. wine vinegar
   ²⁄₃ cup olive oil or vegetable oil
   1 clove garlic, minced
   1 egg yolk

³⁄₄ tsp. salt
¹⁄₄ tsp. white pepper
6 large mushrooms, sliced
6 lettuce cups or leaves
2 cups shredded lettuce (Boston, romaine, iceberg, and endive work well in combination or separately.)
2 tbs. toasted chopped pecans
1 lemon, sliced, for garnish
6 sprigs parsley, for garnish

Rub the duck inside and out with a mixture of salt, pepper, garlic powder, cayenne, and cumin powder. Roast the duck at 225 degrees for 3–4 hours or more or until the drumstick pulls out easily. Chill the duck.

Pick the meat from the duck, and julienne it.

Make the vinaigrette by combining the mustard, vinegar, olive oil, garlic, egg yolk, salt, and pepper.

In a skillet, combine the duck, mushroom slices, and vinaigrette. Cook the mixture over medium heat until it is thoroughly heated.

Place lettuce cups on serving plates, fill the cups with shredded lettuce, and spoon the hot duck mixture over the lettuce mounds. Sprinkle each salad with 1 teaspoon of chopped pecans. Garnish the salads with lemon slices and parsley.

Serves 6.

Shrimp Dijonnaise

48 medium-sized raw shrimp, peeled and
    lightly floured
¾ cup clarified butter
⅓ cup vermouth
Mustard Sauce:
    4 tbs. Pommery mustard
    4 tbs. Dijon mustard
    6 tbs. horseradish
    1 tbs. minced garlic

1 quart whipping cream reduced to 2⅔
    cups
1 6-oz. box Uncle Ben's Long Grain &
    Wild Rice mix
1 tbs. minced parsley
1 lemon
6 sprigs parsley
18 snow peas, steamed

Sauté the floured shrimp in the clarified butter. Drain the butter. Put the shrimp back on the hot burner, and when hot again, deglaze the pan with the vermouth.

In another pan combine the mustards, horseradish, garlic, and reduced cream. Cook the sauce over low heat for 15 minutes. The consistency of the sauce will be very creamy.

Cook the rice according to the directions on the box.

Just before serving, whisk the minced parsley into the sauce. Add the shrimp-vermouth mixture.

Serve over rice. Garnish with lemon slices, parsley sprigs, and snow peas.

Serves 6.

Chocolate Mousse Pie

7½ oz. chocolate cookies or graham
   crackers, pulverized into crumbs
1 stick butter, melted
1 6-oz. package semisweet chocolate
   chips
¼ cup sugar
1 tsp. butter

½ tbs. heavy cream
2 egg yolks
8 oz. cream cheese, room temperature
2 egg whites
¼ cup sugar
1 tbs. vanilla
1 cup heavy cream, chilled

Combine the cookie or cracker crumbs with 1 stick of melted butter. Pat the mixture into a 10-inch pie pan to form a crust.

Melt the chocolate, ¼ cup of sugar, and 1 teaspoon of butter in the top of a double boiler. Do not stir until the mixture is completely melted. Remove from the heat, and stir in the ½ tablespoon of cream.

While melting the chocolate, cream the egg yolks and cream cheese together. Add the warm chocolate mixture to the egg yolk–cream cheese mixture, and stir until they are completely blended.

In another bowl, whip the egg whites to the soft-peak stage, and then gradually whip in ¼ cup of sugar.

In a third bowl, whip 1 cup of cream, adding the vanilla at the soft-peak stage. Whip until stiff peaks form.

Fold all the ingredients together.

Spoon the mousse into the crust, and chill the pie for several hours.

Serves 8.

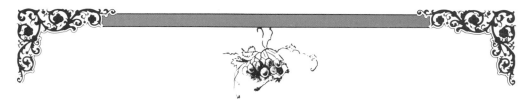

RESTAURANT JONATHAN

714 North Rampart Street

A talented group of men, led by architect Jack Cosner, was formed to finance, create, and operate Restaurant Jonathan—an establishment boasting an authentic Art Deco décor and an exciting menu. The restaurant is located near the Municipal Auditorium and the Theatre for the Performing Arts.

Chef Tom Cowan has worked tirelessly to make Jonathan's kitchen comparable to any in New Orleans. Because of his inventive use of local products, the restaurant has achieved a high level of popularity in the city.

Begun in 1976, it was not until 1978 that Jack Cosner himself actually started to manage and operate the restaurant. The following year he was joined by Michael Morris, who is now sole proprietor of Restaurant Jonathan.

Curry dish with condiments.

Crawfish Jonathan

1 small eggplant, peeled and cut into
  1-inch cubes
2 tbs. salt
1 tbs. bacon grease
1 cup green peppers, diced into ½-inch
  squares
1 cup finely chopped onions
1 small clove garlic, minced
1 cup celery, diced into ½-inch cubes
1 jalapeño pepper, seeds and stem
  removed, minced
½ cup rich shrimp stock (or clam juice,
  oyster water, or fish stock)

¼ cup sherry
½ cup V-8 juice
½ tsp. thyme leaves
¼ tsp. ground black pepper
½ lb. crawfish tails
1 cup unseasoned bread crumbs plus
  extra for topping
¼ tsp. Tabasco
salt to taste
4 tbs. grated Parmesan cheese
butter for topping
½ tsp. paprika

Salt the eggplant with 2 tablespoons of salt, and let it stand for 1 hour. Rinse well, and squeeze dry.

Preheat the oven to 325 degrees.

Heat the bacon grease in a saucepan, and sauté the green peppers, onions, garlic, and celery for 2–3 minutes. Add the eggplant, jalapeño, stock, sherry, V-8 juice, thyme, and black pepper. Cover the pan, or transfer the mixture to a covered baking dish. Bake in the oven for 30 minutes or until the eggplant is done.

Stir in the crawfish tails, and add the bread crumbs. Mix lightly until the liquid is almost all absorbed. The mixture should remain light. Season with Tabasco, and taste for salt.

Put the mixture into individual oven-proof baking dishes or one large soufflé dish. Sprinkle the bread crumbs and Parmesan cheese evenly over the top. Dot with butter and sprinkle with paprika. Heat and serve.

Serves 6.

Black Mushroom Soup

4 quarts water
12 chicken bouillon cubes
1 bunch celery tops, chopped
1 large onion, coarsely chopped
1 bay leaf
2 carrots, coarsely chopped
4 chicken necks

1½ lbs. mushrooms, stems included, finely chopped
¾ cup sherry
¾ cup beef bouillon
¼ tsp. white pepper
¾ cup heavy cream

Make a chicken consommé by putting the water, chicken bouillon cubes, celery tops, onion, bay leaf, carrots, and chicken necks in a soup pot. Bring the stock to a boil, and cook the stock at a simmer for approximately 30 minutes, or until the chicken is tender. Remove the chicken necks. Strain the liquid, put it back into the soup pot, and reduce it by boiling it for 30 minutes. Reserve 7 cups of this reduced consommé.

Put the chopped mushrooms, sherry, and beef bouillon into a 3-quart saucepan. Cook the mixture at a simmer for 15 minutes. Add the reduced chicken consommé and the white pepper. Continue cooking the soup at a simmer for 1 hour.

Just before serving, whip the cream.

Ladle the soup into bowls, and top each serving with whipped cream.

If desired, the cream can be browned under the broiler.

Serves 6–8.

Lamb Curry

7 1/2-lb. leg of lamb with bone
5 cups water
2 celery ribs, quartered
1 small onion, quartered
2 carrots, quartered
2 cloves garlic
4 beef bouillon cubes
1 1/2 tbs. mild or hot curry powder
  (to your taste)
Seasoned Flour:
  3/4 cup flour
  1 1/2 tsp. onion powder
  1 1/2 tsp. salt
  1 1/2 tsp. paprika
  1/2 tsp. dry mustard
  1/4 ground thyme

1/4 tsp. white pepper
1/4 tsp. chili powder
1 cup minced onions
1/2 cup minced celery
1/2 cup minced carrots
1/2 cup minced green peppers
1 tsp. minced garlic
1 or 2 seeded and minced jalapeño
  peppers (to your taste)
1 1/4 cup minced peeled apples
1/2 cup raisins
1/2 cup pineapple juice
1/2 cup apple juice
2 tsp. salt
4 cups cooked rice

Have the leg of lamb boned, and reserve the bone. Place the bone in a soup pot, and cover with the water. Add the celery, onion, carrots, garlic and beef bouillon cubes. Cook partially covered for 2 hours. Strain the stock into a saucepan, and cook it until it is reduced to 1 1/4 cups.

Trim the fat from the lamb, and render the fat in a Dutch oven or heavy pot. Dice the meat into 1-inch pieces, and sprinkle it with curry powder. Dredge the meat in seasoned flour, and brown the meat in the fat over medium heat for about 10 minutes. Remove the meat, and set it aside. Add the minced onions, celery, carrots, peppers, garlic, jalapeño peppers, and apples to the Dutch oven or pot, and sauté the mixture over medium heat for 5 minutes. Stir in the raisins, fruit juices, and lamb stock, and stir constantly for 5 minutes to deglaze the pot. Return the meat to the pot, cover, and simmer gently for 30 minutes or until the meat is tender. Season the curry with 2 teaspoons of salt.

Serve 1 cup of lamb curry with 2/3 cup of cooked rice per person. Restaurant Jonathan suggests the following garnishes be served on a tray to accompany the curry: sliced bananas, sliced pineapple, coconut, raisins, chopped nuts, chopped crisp bacon, and sliced cherry tomatoes.

Serves 6.

Fresh Asparagus
with Lemon-Chive Butter

2 large bunches asparagus
2 quarts water
1 tbs. salt
½ lb. or 2 sticks butter
2 tsp. lemon juice

½ tsp. onion powder
½ cup fresh chopped chives (or green
    onion tops, finely chopped)
2 dashes Tabasco

Wash and trim the asparagus.

Bring to a boil the water, which has been seasoned with the salt. Cook the asparagus for 5–7 minutes or until the asparagus are tender.

While cooking the asparagus, melt the butter in a saucepan, and add the lemon juice, onion powder, chives, and Tabasco.

Arrange the cooked asparagus on a warm plate, and pour the lemon-chive butter sauce over the vegetable.

Serves 6.

Chef Tom Cowan.

Watercress, Bacon, and Mushroom Salad

2 bunches watercress
8 slices bacon
1 lb. firm, white mushrooms
juice from 1 lemon
1 stale crust of bread
2 cloves garlic
1 tsp. salt
1 tsp. dry mustard
1 tsp. black pepper

1 tsp. sugar
2 tsp. Dijon mustard
¾ cup olive oil
4 tbs. vinegar (white or red)
splash of Worcestershire sauce
2 tbs. onion powder
2–3 egg yolks, sieved (optional)
cherry tomatoes, halved, for garnish

Wash and trim the stems from the watercress, then pat dry. Wrap the watercress in a towel, and put it in the refrigerator until ready to use.

Cook the bacon until it is crisp. Drain, finely chop, and reserve it for topping.

Wash, trim, and slice the mushrooms. Toss with the lemon juice.

To make the vinaigrette, rub the crust of bread with the peeled garlic cloves, and put it in the bottom of a bowl. Stir in the salt, dry mustard, pepper, sugar, Dijon mustard, olive oil, vinegar, Worcestershire sauce, and onion powder. When ready to serve the salad, remove the garlic crouton and toss the watercress and mushrooms in the dressing.

Serve the salad on chilled plates. Sprinkle the reserved chopped bacon on top and, if desired, some sieved hard-cooked egg yolks. Garnish the salads with a few cherry tomatoes sliced in half.

Serves 6.

Almond Amaretto Mousse

1 cup sugar
1 stick butter
4 egg yolks
½ cup half-and-half
2 tbs. amaretto
½ tsp. vanilla extract

1 tsp. almond extract
2 tbs. lemon juice
1 pint (2 cups) heavy cream, chilled
4 egg whites, room temperature
2–3 tbs. toasted, sliced almonds

In a heavy saucepan combine the sugar, butter, and egg yolks. Stirring this mixture constantly, bring it to a boil and continue to boil it for 2 minutes. Remove the mixture from the heat, and strain it into a bowl. To quickly chill the mixture, place the bowl in a larger bowl filled with ice. Stir until the mixture is cool. When cool, add the amaretto, vanilla and almond extracts, and lemon juice. Mix well.

In another bowl whip the heavy cream until stiff peaks form. Be careful not to overbeat. Fold the whipped cream into the cooled mixture. (Reserve a small amount of the whipped cream for the topping.)

In another bowl whip the egg whites until stiff peaks form, being careful not to overbeat. Carefully fold the whipped egg whites into the above mixture.

Fill dessert glasses with the mousse. Chill the mousse for several hours before serving.

To serve, top each portion with a spoonful of whipped cream and a sprinkling of toasted almonds.

Serves 6.

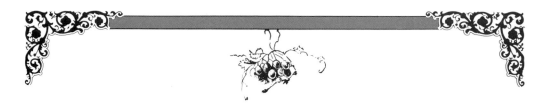

RIB ROOM

Royal Orleans Hotel
621 St. Louis Street

When the elegant Royal Orleans Hotel was built, the owners wanted to create a restaurant that would offer an alternative to the typical cuisines of New Orleans. Since its opening in 1961, the Rib Room has become a most popular local dining spot. Specializing in serving the finest aged prime ribs of beef, the restaurant has given us that needed alternative. The English-style décor is highlighted by huge arched windows overlooking Royal Street and the endless parade of passers-by. Open, airy, and masculine-looking in design, the room is a favorite luncheon place for local businessmen.

Andrea Apuzzo, executive chef of the Royal Orleans, maintains a menu of delicious offerings of the highest quality.

Escargot à la Louisiane

36 large fresh mushrooms
1 cup white vinegar
3 tbs. butter
2 tbs. finely chopped French shallots
1 cup water
¾ cup white wine
2 tbs. lemon juice
1 tsp. finely chopped garlic
36 escargots
4 tbs. brandy
2½ cups heavy cream

1 tsp. cornstarch
½ tsp. salt
¼ tsp. white pepper
Hollandaise Sauce:
   3 egg yolks
   2 tbs. lemon juice
   ¼ tsp. salt
   pinch of cayenne
   1 stick butter
1 tbs. chopped parsley

Remove the stems from the mushrooms, and set them aside for use in another dish. Soak the caps in the vinegar for 5 minutes.

Melt 1 tablespoon of butter in a skillet. Add 1 tablespoon of shallots, and sauté until the shallots are golden. Add the mushrooms, water, ½ cup of wine, and 2 tablespoons of lemon juice, and simmer gently for 25 minutes.

In a separate skillet, melt the remaining 2 tablespoons of butter, and sauté the remaining 1 tablespoon of shallots and the garlic until they turn light brown. Add the escargots, and sauté for 3 minutes. Pour the brandy over the escargots, and flame. When the flame dies down, stir in ¼ cup of wine, and simmer for 5 minutes until the wine is reduced. There should be just enough liquid to cover the bottom of the pan. Remove the escargots from the skillet, and set them aside. Add the heavy cream to the skillet, and cook the sauce over low heat until it is reduced to medium thickness (about 20–30 minutes). If the sauce is not thick enough, add the cornstarch (dissolved in 1 teaspoon of water) and bring the sauce to a simmer to thicken. Season the cream sauce with ½ teaspoon of salt and the pepper.

Make the hollandaise by blending the egg yolks, 2 tablespoons of lemon juice, ¼ teaspoon of salt, and cayenne in a blender on medium speed for a few seconds.

Heat 1 stick of butter to a bubbling boil, but do not brown. With the blender on high speed, pour the hot butter into the other ingredients in a slow, steady stream. When all the butter has been added, blend a few seconds more.

Place the mushroom caps in individual escargot plates or in a baking pan. Stuff each mushroom cap with an escargot, and cover with the cream sauce. Top each escargot with 1 teaspoon of hollandaise sauce.

Place the dish under the broiler until the hollandaise is lightly browned. Sprinkle the dish with chopped parsley, and serve.

Serves 6.

Butterfly Fillets Pontchatoula

6 7-oz. beef fillets
3 tbs. oil
1 stick butter
3 tbs. chopped French shallots
1 tbs. chopped garlic
2 cups fresh sliced mushrooms
6 oz. raw peeled shrimp
⅔ cup diced green peppers
⅔ cup diced red peppers
⅓ cup brandy

Brown Sauce:
  6 tbs. flour
  4 tbs. butter
  2 cups beef stock (bouillon or canned is
    fine)
½ tsp. crushed black peppercorns
½ cup whipping cream
salt to taste
pepper to taste
1 tbs. chopped parsley

Cut the fillets horizontally almost all the way through, and open them up to resemble butterflies. In a large skillet, heat enough oil to cover the bottom, and pan-fry the fillets to individual taste. Remove the fillets from the pan, and set them aside. Drain the oil from the pan, and return the pan to the heat. Add 1 stick of butter, the shallots, and the garlic to the pan, and sauté the mixture over medium heat for 2 minutes. Add the mushrooms, shrimp, and red and green peppers to the pan, and sauté the mixture 15–20 minutes more. Return the fillets to the pan, pour in the brandy, and flame. When the flame dies down, remove the fillets and keep them warm until serving time.

To make the brown sauce, melt 4 tablespoons of butter in a saucepan. Add the flour, and stir over medium-low heat until the roux turns medium brown. Be careful not to burn the roux. Remove the roux from the heat, and gradually add the beef stock, stirring to avoid lumps. Return the sauce to the heat, and bring it to a boil, stirring constantly. Remove the pan from the heat, and season the sauce to taste.

Add the peppercorns, brown sauce, and cream to the sautéed ingredients, and cook the sauce over low heat until it is thickened and creamy. Season the sauce with salt and pepper.

Lay the fillets on serving plates, and top with the sauce. Garnish each fillet with ½ tsp. parsley. The Rib Room suggests an accompaniment of rice pilaf (see the following recipe), steamed asparagus, and a peeled cherry tomato to garnish.

Serves 6.

Clockwise from right: Butterfly Fillets Pontchatoula, Rib Room Salad, Chocolate Mousse, Escargot à la Louisiane.

Rice Pilaf

½ cup chopped onions
2 tbs. butter
1 cup uncooked rice
1½ cups chicken stock or bouillon

1 bay leaf
¼ tsp. black pepper
salt to taste

Sauté the onions in the butter for 2 minutes.

In a baking pan mix together the sautéed onions, rice, chicken stock, bay leaf, pepper, and salt. Cover the pan. Bake at 375 degrees for 30 minutes. Remove the pan from the oven, fluff the rice with a fork, and cook 10 minutes more, uncovered.

Serves 4.

House Salad and Dressing

House Dressing:
   1 egg
   1½ cups olive oil
   ½ cup red wine vinegar
   1 tsp. salt
   ¼ tsp. black pepper
   ½ tsp. sugar
   ½ tsp. Coleman's dry English mustard
   ⅛ tsp. Worcestershire sauce
   6–8 drops Tabasco

   ½ cup crumbled Roquefort cheese
   1 quart cleaned, torn mixed greens (iceberg lettuce, romaine, and chickory in equal parts)
   ¾ cup croutons (made by cutting toast into ½-inch cubes and frying them in butter)
   ½ cup sliced green onions

Mix the egg and olive oil in a blender. Add the vinegar, salt, pepper, sugar, mustard, Worcestershire sauce, and Tabasco, and blend. Slowly mix in the cheese.

Toss the greens together with the dressing and croutons. Sprinkle the sliced green onions on top.

Serves 8.

Chocolate Mousse

8½ oz. semisweet chocolate
½ tsp. vanilla
pinch of salt
2 egg whites
¼ cup sugar

2½ cups heavy cream
2 egg yolks
shaved chocolate, for garnish
powdered sugar, for garnish

Melt the chocolate in the top of a double boiler. Stir in the vanilla and salt. Set the mixture aside to cool slightly.

Whip the egg whites with the sugar until stiff peaks form.

Whip the cream until stiff peaks form.

Blend the egg yolks into the melted chocolate. Gently fold in the whipped cream and egg whites.

Spoon the mixture into individual dessert dishes, and refrigerate the desserts for at least 2 hours before serving.

Garnish each serving with shaved chocolate and powdered sugar.

Serves 6–8.

Dessert cart.

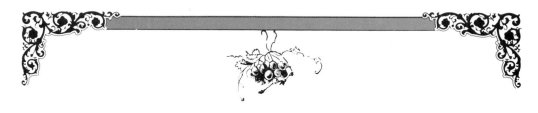

SAZERAC

Fairmont Hotel
123 Baronne Street

In 1859 John B. Schiller opened a bar in Exchange Alley called the Sazerac Coffee House, which he named after the French cognac he served there—Sazerac-de-Forge. His cognac cocktails became very popular, particularly his cocktail of cognac and Peychaud bitters. The bar changed hands and became the Sazerac House, and the drink changed, too—absinthe was added, and the Sazerac-de-Forge cognac was substituted with rye whiskey.

In 1949 owners of the Roosevelt Hotel purchased exclusive rights to the Sazerac cocktail, and the hotel bar was named the Sazerac.

When the Fairmont Corporation purchased the Roosevelt, they wanted a magnificent dining room. Thus was born in 1973 the Sazerac Restaurant. The room boasts plush red damask walls, black enamel trim, and huge gilt rococo frames surrounding portraits of historic Louisiana figures. The classic elegance and creative combination of local and continental fare have made the Sazerac a popular New Orleans experience.

Sazerac Cocktail

The following is touted to be the original recipe from the Sazerac House.

1 tsp. sugar	1½ oz. rye whiskey
1 dash Peychaud bitters	1 dash Herbsaint or absinthe substitute
1 dash Angostura bitters	1 twist lemon peel

Pack one 3½-ounce Old Fashioned glass with crushed ice.

In another Old Fashioned glass blend the sugar, Peychaud and Angostura bitters, and the rye whiskey until the sugar is dissolved. Add a cube or two of ice, and stir.

Sazerac Cocktail.

Take the first glass, discard the ice, and drop in a dash of Herbsaint. Twirl the glass to coat the inside with Herbsaint, and pour out any liquid remaining in the bottom.

Pour the blended cocktail into this glass. Twist a lemon peel over the cocktail, but don't drop it into the glass.

Serves 1.

Crab Claws Ambassador

1 stick butter	60 Louisiana crab claws
½ tsp. finely chopped garlic	½ tsp. salt
½ cup finely chopped onions	¼ tsp. freshly ground pepper
¼ cup chopped parsley	3 tbs. Courvoisier or brandy
2 tsp. Creole mustard	

Melt the butter in a large skillet, and sauté the garlic, onions, parsley, and mustard for 5–7 minutes. Do not brown. Add the crab claws, and simmer for 5 minutes, turning them gently until they are well coated with the butter mixture and evenly heated. Season the claws with salt and pepper. Pour the Courvoisier or brandy over the claws, and flame.

Serve immediately.

Serves 6.

Clockwise from top: Soufflé Grand Marnier with Raspberry Sauce, Crab Claws Ambassador, Fruits of the Bayou Vol-au-Vent, Spinach Salad.

Spinach Salad

2 10-oz. packages fresh spinach
10 strips bacon
½ tsp. rosemary
½ tsp. tarragon
½ tsp. orégano
4 tbs. olive oil
6 tbs. red wine vinegar

2 tsp. Worcestershire sauce
2 tsp. Dijon mustard
4 tsp. sugar
¼ tsp. freshly ground black pepper, or
   to taste
¼ tsp. salt, or to taste

Remove the stems from the spinach, and wash the spinach well. Drain the spinach thoroughly in a colander, and set it aside.

Cut the bacon into 1-inch pieces, and fry the bacon in a skillet until the pieces are crisp. Drain the bacon on paper towels, and remove the excess grease from the skillet. Add the rosemary, tarragon, and orégano to the skillet. Add the oil, vinegar, Worcestershire sauce, mustard, and sugar. Mix well. Allow the mixture to simmer for 3 minutes. Add the pepper and salt. Remove the skillet from the heat.

186

Transfer the spinach to a large bowl, and pour the hot dressing over the greens. Cover the bowl, and shake it to distribute the dressing evenly over the spinach. Leaving the bowl covered, allow the spinach to steam for about 15 seconds.

Crumble the bacon over the salad, and toss. Serve the salad immediately.

Serves 6.

Fruits of the Bayou Vol-au-Vent

1 stick butter
¾ cup flour
1 cup minced French shallots or green onions
¼ cup minced green pepper
¼ cup minced celery
1 tbs. minced garlic
3 cups milk, warmed
3 cups fish stock (use 2 cups water in which shrimp have been parboiled plus 1 cup oyster liquor—see below)
¼ cup white wine

⅛ tsp. thyme
1½ tsp. salt
1 tsp. white pepper
1 cup sliced mushrooms
4 doz. fresh oysters, drained (reserve 1 cup liquor)
1 cup parboiled and peeled shrimp, diced
1 cup lump crabmeat
1 large, prepared vol-au-vent or 6 prepared patty shells
1 tsp. minced parsley

In a large skillet, melt the butter. Stir in the flour, and cook the roux over low heat for about 5 minutes. Add the shallots or green onions, green pepper, celery, and garlic, stirring until well blended with the white roux. Cook the mixture an additional 5 minutes until the vegetables become limp, taking care not to brown the mixture. Stir in the warmed milk and fish stock gradually to avoid lumps. Cook until the mixture has thickened. Stir in the white wine, thyme, salt, and pepper. Fold in the mushrooms and seafood, and simmer gently for about 20 minutes or until the seafood is cooked and the white sauce is thick.

Pour the mixture into a baked vol-au-vent, or divide it into six baked patty shells. Sprinkle the vol-au-vent or each patty shell with chopped parsley, and cover with a pastry lid.

Serves 6.

Soufflé Grand Marnier

2 tbs. butter
2 tbs. flour
1 cup milk
1 cup sugar

grated rind of ½ orange
7 egg yolks
3 tbs. Grand Marnier
7 egg whites

Preheat the oven to 375 degrees.

Melt the butter, and pour it into a large mixing bowl. Add the flour, and make a paste.

In a saucepan, bring the milk, ½ cup of sugar, and the orange rind to a boil. Gradually add this to the paste. Let this mixture cool slightly. Beat the egg yolks into the above mixture by hand one at a time. Add the Grand Marnier.

Place the egg whites and ¼ cup sugar in a separate mixing bowl, and beat at high speed with an electric mixer. Gradually add another ¼ cup sugar, and continue beating until the egg whites form stiff peaks.

Gently fold the egg whites into the other ingredients. Pour the mixture into six individual buttered and sugared soufflé molds. Bake the soufflés in the oven for about 15 minutes or until the tops are lightly browned. Serve immediately.

Serves 6.

SBISA'S

1011 Decatur Street

Larry Hill is a child psychiatrist and restaurateur. He has always been interested in good food and the good life in New Orleans. Raised primarily by his grandmother and great aunt, both of whom were Alsatian and ran wonderful European kitchens in their homes, he was always exposed to good food. It was a major part of his family's life style. In his household it was a tradition that men cooked.

His great uncle, by whom he was strongly influenced, would do all the marketing for the family. As a child Larry would go to the French Market with his uncle and would buy vegetables. Next he and his uncle would go to Solari's and buy delicacies for the family breakfast. Everything would be delivered later in the day. They would then go home, where the first major meal of the day was breakfast, served at noon.

Larry always liked to cook. As his medical career got under way, cooking and entertaining became an important part of his life. So important was his interest in food that Larry decided to open a restaurant, Marti's, with Martin Shambra.

Larry ran the restaurant for four years, then sold his interest to his partner and went into psychiatry full time. But he missed the restaurant business and decided to open a new restaurant. Larry asked his friend John Pico to become a partner, and together in 1979 they bought Sbisa's Café on Decatur Street. Café Sbisa had been a restaurant since about 1899 but had declined to a point that the kitchen was closed and only drinks and an occasional oyster were served. On purchase of the property, Larry and John closed the business and began an extensive renovation, restoring the building to its original beauty and purpose. The concept of the restaurant began to develop. The result was a sort of New Orleans–style French grill. The specialties include charcoal-grilled seafood, both local and from other areas of the country, and lighter versions of traditional New Orleans fare. Sbisa's is perhaps the only restaurant in the city to serve fresh clams and mussels on the half shell.

Chef Jason Clevinger prepares specials several times a week so that he may offer new and different dishes to Sbisa's patrons.

The restaurant's atmosphere is relaxed and friendly. There is piano music and an upstairs bar that overlooks the dining room. Café Sbisa has quickly become a regular dining place for locals and visitors alike.

189

Yellow Squash and Shrimp Bisque

1 lb. yellow squash, sliced
2 quarts water
6 tbs. (¾ stick) butter
⅓ cup flour
⅓ cup chopped onion
⅓ cup chopped bell pepper
⅓ cup chopped celery
¼ tsp. white pepper
¼ tsp. cayenne

½ tsp. powdered thyme
2 bay leaves
1 chicken bouillon cube
½ tsp. salt
½ lb. raw peeled, deveined shrimp, chopped (approximately 11 oz. unpeeled, heads on)
½ cup heavy cream

Boil the sliced yellow squash in the water for 25 minutes. Reserving the liquid, strain the squash in a colander. Purée the squash.

Melt the butter in a 3-quart saucepan, and stir in the flour. Whisk the roux over medium heat until it is golden, approximately 6–7 minutes. Add the onion, bell pepper, and celery. Sauté the mixture for 5 minutes. Add the puréed squash, reserved liquid, white pepper, cayenne, thyme, bay leaves, chicken bouillon cube, and salt. Simmer the mixture for 20 minutes. Add the chopped shrimp and heavy cream. Simmer the bisque for 10 minutes more. Correct the seasonings, and serve.

Serves 6.

Artichokes with Crabmeat
and Green Mayonnaise

6 quarts water
6 tbs. salt
1 lemon, halved
1 tbs. olive oil
6 artichokes, stems cut off
1 lb. good lump crabmeat
2 lemons, quartered, for garnish
Green Mayonnaise:
    1 egg
    1⅓ tbs. Poupon (Dijon) mustard

2½ tbs. tarragon vinegar
2¾ tbs. minced parsley
2¾ tbs. minced green onions
¾ tsp. white pepper
¼ tsp. salt
2¼ tsp. dried tarragon or 1 tsp. minced fresh tarragon
1⅓ tbs. dried basil or ¼ cup chopped, loosely packed fresh basil
1 cup vegetable oil

To the water add the salt, squeeze in the lemon juice, and add the squeezed lemon halves and the olive oil. Bring the water to a boil, and add the artichokes. Boil the artichokes for 40–45 minutes or until they are done. Remove the artichokes from the water, and let them cool.

Prepare the green mayonnaise. Place the egg, mustard, vinegar, parsley, green onions, pepper, salt, tarragon, and basil in a blender, and purée. With the blender on, pour in the oil in a thin stream until you have added the full cup.

Remove the leaves from the artichokes. Save 8 nice ones for each serving, 48 leaves altogether. Cut out the hairy choke, and discard it.

For final assembly, arrange 8 artichoke leaves in a circle on each plate. Place an artichoke bottom in the center of the plate, top with the crabmeat, and spoon ¼ cup of green mayonnaise on each.

Serves 6.

Clockwise from top: Yellow Squash and Shrimp Bisque, Artichokes with Crabmeat and Green Mayonnaise, Grilled Redfish with Sauce Criolla, Susan's Chocolate Cake.

Grilled Redfish with Sauce Criolla

6 skinned redfish fillets, 8½–9 oz. each,
  ½ inch to 1 inch thick
vegetable oil
2 tbs. butter
Sauce Criolla:

    ½ lb. fresh tomatoes, peeled and seeded
    ½ cucumber, unpeeled, seeded and
      chopped
    ½ bell pepper, seeded and chopped
    ½ yellow onion, chopped

1½ cloves garlic, peeled and minced
2 tsp. capers, drained
½ tsp. tarragon, minced
¼ cup chopped parsley
2 tbs. Poupon mustard
1½ tbs. wine vinegar
3 tsp. olive oil
¼ tsp. salt
½ tsp. cayenne

Light the grill or barbecue pit 1 hour before cooking. The grill must be very clean or the fish will stick to it and collect the ash.

Prepare the Sauce Criolla. Put the tomatoes, cucumber, bell pepper, onion, garlic, capers, tarragon, parsley, mustard, vinegar, olive oil, salt, and cayenne in a food processor. Pulse the machine so that everything is blended but not puréed. The vegetables should still be crunchy. This sauce or relish should be peppery hot and served at room temperature.

Trim the redfish fillets so that the ends are squared off. This is done to achieve an attractive presentation. (The trimmings may be used for fish stock, fish pâté, or fish chips.)

Brush the grill with oil. Brush the rounded side of the redfish fillets with oil. This helps prevent the fish from sticking or drying out during cooking. Place the fillets on the grill rounded side down. Watch the end of the redfish. When the fish are half white, oil the top of the fish and turn them. The fish will cook at 10 minutes per 1 inch of thickness.

When the fish are done, remove them and place them on serving plates. Top each fillet with a teaspoon of butter.

Serve with the Sauce Criolla on the side.

Serves 6.

Susan's Chocolate Cake

1 cup flour
1 cup sugar
¼ tsp. salt
½ stick butter
½ cup water
¼ cup shortening
1½ tbs. powdered cocoa
1 egg beaten
½ tsp. baking soda
¼ cup buttermilk
½ tsp. vanilla

Icing:
   ½ stick butter
   1½ tbs. powdered cocoa
   ½ pound (½ box) powdered sugar
   ½ tsp. vanilla
   ¼ cup chopped pecans
   pinch of salt
   3 tbs. milk
Whipped Cream Topping:
   1 cup heavy cream
   1 tbs. powdered sugar
   1 tsp. vanilla

Preheat the oven to 350 degrees.

Sift the flour, sugar, and ¼ teaspoon of salt together into a bowl.

Put ½ stick of butter, water, shortening, and 1½ tablespoons of cocoa in a 1½-quart saucepan. Bring the mixture to a boil. Stir in the flour-sugar-salt mixture. Mix well. Add the egg, baking soda, buttermilk, and ½ teaspoon of vanilla to the saucepan. Remove the batter from the heat, and pour it into an 8½ by 12 by 1-inch jellyroll or baking pan. Bake the cake in the oven for 20 minutes or until a knife inserted into the middle of the cake comes out clean.

While the cake bakes, make the icing. In a small saucepan melt ½ stick of butter, and blend in 1½ tablespoons of cocoa. Do not boil. Remove the pan from the heat, and stir in ½ pound of powdered sugar, ½ teaspoon of vanilla, the pecans, a pinch of salt, and the milk. Mix well.

When the cake is done, pour the icing over the top and let the cake cool.

In a bowl, whip the cream together with 1 tablespoon of powdered sugar and 1 teaspoon of vanilla unitl stiff peaks form.

Cut the cake into six equal portions, and serve it at room temperature topped with the whipped cream.

Serves 6.

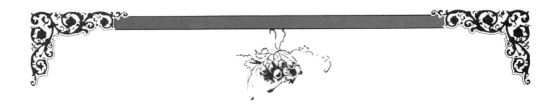

STEPHEN & MARTIN

1613 Milan Street

Having started in 1945 as a neighborhood restaurant, Stephen & Martin was transformed in 1975 into one of New Orleans' major restaurants. From the Oyster Bar in the cheery, gardenish dining room to the bilevel discothèque to the new dining room on St. Charles Avenue where one can watch the last of the charming street-cars clang by, Stephen & Martin is unique to New Orleans. The menu is a creative blend of Creole and Italian cuisines produced daily under the direction of James "Beany" McGregor. The following recipes are a few of his works.

Shrimp St. James

1 lb. medium-small shrimp with shells and heads removed and reserved
2 cups water
¼ lemon
½ tsp. salt
⅛ tsp. pepper
dash Tabasco
4 large artichokes
2 tbs. salt
6 tbs. butter
6 tbs. flour
⅓ cup chopped onions
¼ cup chopped celery
⅓ cup chopped bell pepper
1½ tsp. minced garlic

¾ cup chopped parsley
1 cup sliced green onions (white and green parts)
¼ cup dry sherry
½ tsp. ground thyme
salt to taste
¼ tsp. white pepper
½ tsp. Worcestershire sauce
1 tsp. lemon juice
⅛ tsp. Tabasco
¼ tsp. sugar
2 tbs. grated Romano cheese
2 tbs. bread crumbs
6 slices lemon
paprika

Boil the shrimp shells and heads in the water, to which ¼ of a lemon, ½ teaspoon of salt, the pepper, and a dash of Tabasco have been added. Cook for 20–30 minutes, and strain. Reserve ¾ cup of stock. (If shrimp heads are not available, put the shrimp in lightly seasoned water, bring the water to a boil, and boil the shrimp for 1 minute. Use that water for the stock. Be sure to add the shrimp at the very end of the recipe to avoid their overcooking.)

Boil the artichokes in water to cover which has been seasoned with 2 tablespoons of salt. Cook the artichokes until they are tender. Reserve ¼ cup of the liquid, and add it to the reserved shrimp stock. Set the liquid aside. Dice the artichoke hearts when they are cool, and reserve them.

Make a roux by melting the butter over medium heat and mixing it with the flour, stirring constantly until the mixture is golden (approximately 7–8 minutes).

Add the chopped onions, celery, bell pepper, garlic, and parsley, and cook 5–6 minutes longer. Add the shrimp-artichoke stock, the diced artichoke hearts, and the shrimp. Cook the mixture for 2–3 minutes or until the shrimp have lost their water. Add the green onions, sherry, thyme, white pepper, Worcestershire sauce, lemon juice, ⅛ teaspoon of Tabasco, and sugar. Cook 5 minutes more. Let the mixture cool.

Spoon the mixture into six small ramekins. Mix the Romano cheese with the bread crumbs. Top each ramekin with this mixture, place a slice of lemon on top, and sprinkle with paprika. Put the ramekins in a 350-degree oven for 15–20 minutes.

Serves 6.

Exterior of Stephen & Martin. Club 4141 is at the left.

Split Pea Soup

1 1/2 cups finely minced onions
   (approximately 2 large onions)
3/4 cup diced ham (approximately 1/4 lb.)
3 tbs. vegetable oil
2 cups split peas
1 ham bone
12 cups hot tap water

1/2 cup chicken stock or bouillon
1 1/2 tsp. sugar
1 1/4 tsp. salt
1/2 tsp. black pepper
1/4 tsp. Tabasco
1 cup diced potatoes (optional)
1 cup diced carrots (optional)

In a soup pot sauté the onions and ham in the vegetable oil until the onions are translucent, about 2–3 minutes. Add the split peas, ham bone, water, and stock or bouillon. Cook the soup over medium to medium-high heat for 50–55 minutes or until the soup is smooth. Add the sugar, salt, pepper, and Tabasco.

If you add the potatoes and carrots, put them in the pot for the last 25 minutes of cooking time.

Serves 6.

Avocado, Cucumber, Onion,
and Tomato Salad

House Dressing:
   3/4 cup olive oil
   1/2 cup plus 1 tbs. vegetable oil
   3 tbs. red wine vinegar
   1 tsp. sugar
   1 tsp. salt
   2 tsp. basil
   2 tsp. orégano
   1/2 tsp. lemon juice
   1/4 tsp. black pepper
   1/2 tbs. chopped parsley
   pinch of garlic powder
   1/4 tsp. grated Romano cheese

   a few drops Worcestershire sauce
   1/2 small egg
6 large leaves romaine or leaf lettuce
6 cups torn iceberg lettuce
2 cups sliced ripe avocado
3 medium Creole tomatoes or regular
   tomatoes, each sliced into eighths
2 cups red onions, sliced into rings
1 medium cucumber, sliced
1 small head cauliflower (to yield 24
   florets), blanched in boiling water

Place all the ingredients for the house dressing in a blender or food processor, and blend or process them for 1 minute. Refrigerate the dressing before using it.

Line six salad bowls with the romaine or leaf lettuce. Top with the torn iceberg lettuce. Prepare the other vegetables, and arrange them in an attractive manner over the lettuce.

Top each salad with ¼ cup of the house dressing.

Serves 6.

Clockwise from top: Snap Beans; Veal Esplanade; Shrimp St. James; Split Pea Soup; Avocado, Cucumber, Onion, and Tomato Salad; Almond Torte; French Bread.

Veal Esplanade

Béchamel Sauce:
  4 tbs. butter
  4 tbs. flour
  1¼ cups milk
  ½ cup chicken stock or bouillon
  1 tbs. sherry
  ½ tsp. salt or to taste
  ⅛ tsp. white pepper
  pinch cayenne
  1 egg yolk
Crabmeat Stuffing:
  3 tbs. finely chopped onion
  4 tbs. finely chopped celery
  ⅓ cup finely chopped bell pepper
  1 tsp. minced garlic
  ⅓ cup finely chopped parsley
  2 tbs. butter
  1 lb. lump crabmeat

4½ cups cubed stale French bread soaked
  in enough water to make a mass
⅓ cup sliced green onions (white and
  green parts)
1 tsp. salt
¼ tsp. black pepper
⅛ tsp. ground thyme
4 tsp. lemon juice
1 tbs. brown sugar
1½ tbs. seasoned bread crumbs
12 2½-oz. medallions of milk-fed rib-eye
veal
2 eggs, lightly beaten
1½ cups milk
1 cup flour
peanut oil for frying

To make the béchamel, melt 4 tablespoons of butter in a saucepan, and stir in 4 tablespoons of flour. Cook the roux over medium heat, stirring constantly, until the mixture turns golden, approximately 7–8 minutes. Combine 1¼ cups of milk and the stock in another saucepan. Warm the mixture, and add this to the roux. Cook the sauce for 1 minute, stirring. Add the sherry, salt, white pepper, and cayenne, and mix well. Remove the sauce from the heat, cool slightly, then add the egg yolk while stirring vigorously. Reserve ⅓ cup of the béchamel for the crabmeat stuffing, the rest for the veal.

To make the crabmeat stuffing, sauté the chopped onion, celery, bell pepper, garlic, and parsley in 2 tablespoons of butter for 3–4 minutes. When the garlic begins to brown, add the crabmeat and French bread. Cook the mixture over low heat for 15–20 minutes, stirring constantly. During this step, you may need to add up to ⅓ cup of water to loosen the mixture. Add the green onions, pepper, thyme, lemon juice, brown sugar, ⅓ cup of the reserved béchamel sauce, and the bread crumbs, and cook 3–4 minutes more. Let the stuffing cool. (If the stuffing is not to be used immediately, store it in the refrigerator. Return the stuffing to room temperature before preparing the veal.)

Pound the medallions between two sheets of plastic wrap with a rolling pin until the veal is very thin. Stuff each medallion with approximately 3–4 tablespoons of stuffing, placing the stuffing an inch from one end of the veal and rolling up that end to contain the stuffing. Turn in the outside edges of the veal to seal the stuffing. Finally, roll up the remaining length of the veal. (This is the same procedure used in forming an eggroll.) Secure the veal with a toothpick.

Dip each veal roll into the eggs, which have been beaten lightly with 1 1/2 cups of milk. Then dredge the veal in 1 cup of flour.

Deep-fry the veal rolls in peanut oil that has been heated to 375 degrees. Cook the veal until the stuffing is hot in the center (about 2–3 minutes) and the veal nicely browned.

Drain the veal rolls. Place two veal rolls on each of six plates. Top each serving with approximately 1/4 cup of the reserved béchamel sauce.

Serves 6.

Snap Beans

1 lb. snap beans
1/4 cup (approximately 3 slices) diced bacon
1 stick butter
1 cup diced onions

2 cups sliced fresh mushrooms
1/2 cup brown sugar
1/2 tsp. salt
1/2 tsp. black pepper
1 1/2 tsp. Worcestershire sauce

Lightly steam the beans until they are cooked but still crisp.

Meanwhile, cook the bacon in a frying pan until it is lightly browned. Add the butter to the bacon. After the butter has melted, add the remaining ingredients to the frying pan, and cook the mixture for 2–3 minutes until the onions are transparent. Pour the mixture over the beans, and serve.

Serves 6.

Almond Torte

2 sticks butter, softened
½ cup sugar
1⅔ cups packed brown sugar
1 egg
1 tbs. almond extract

1½ cups sliced almonds, roasted at
  350 degrees until golden brown
  (approximately 15 minutes)
whipped cream for topping

Cream the butter and sugar in a mixing bowl. Gradually add the brown sugar. Cream in the egg, almond extract, and 1 cup of the roasted almonds. Whip the batter with a mixer for 15 minutes on high speed. Turn the mixture into a pan lined with plastic wrap, cover, and freeze for 1 hour.

Shape the mixture into a log 2½ inches in diameter. Roll the log in ¼ cup of the roasted almonds and refreeze it.

To serve, cut the log into ½-inch slices, and place each slice onto a serving plate. Garnish each slice with a dollop of whipped cream. Divide the remaining ¼ cup of almonds among the portions to garnish.

Serves 6–8.

TCHOUPITOULAS PLANTATION

6535 River Road
Avondale, Louisiana

Norma Wallace, a famous New Orleans madame, bought the Tchoupitoulas Plantation in the early 1950s and operated it as an elegant brothel until 1963, when the
Tchoupitoulas Restaurant opened. She sold the restaurant in 1968. It was again
sold in 1977 to Emile Genarro.

Emile's wife and son Charles ran the restaurant until the elder Genarros retired
and Charles took over. Charles's grandfather owned and operated a small
neighborhood restaurant called Genarro's. It was here that the family learned its
trade.

Tchoupitoulas Plantation actually was a plantation and still maintains the atmosphere of one. However, the restaurant retains some remembrances of Norma's
period such as the seven nudes gracing the walls of one dining room.

As in most family operations, Charles has learned the business from being in the
business—relying on the exchange received from customers just as customers rely
on his abilities as a restaurateur.

A recent popular concoction of Charles's is his Jezebel Cocktail, the name being in
keeping with the history of Tchoupitoulas.

Jezebel Cocktail. Mix together in a shaker 2 ounces of apricot
brandy, 1 1/2 ounces of dark rum, 2 ounces of orange juice, 2
ounces of lemon juice, and 4 ounces of green passion fruit liquid,
and pour over crushed ice. Add 3/4 ounce of blackberry brandy,
but do not stir. Garnish with a cherry and an orange slice.

201

Oysters Tchoupitoulas

1 quart oysters
2 quarts water
4 chicken bouillon cubes
3 bay leaves
1 5-oz. bottle of A.1. Sauce

1½ sticks of butter
1 cup plus 2 tbs. flour
¾ cup finely chopped green onions
   (white and green parts)
¼ cup red wine

Poach the oysters in the water until they are firm. Add the bouillon cubes, bay leaves, and A.1. Sauce. Turn off the heat.

In a small saucepan, melt the butter and stir in the flour. Cook the roux over medium-low heat until it turns medium brown (approximately 20–25 minutes). Add the green onions to the roux, and sauté the mixture for 1 minute. Add this mixture to the oyster broth. Add the red wine, and simmer the mixture for 20 minutes.

Serves 8.

Trout Creole

6 4–6-oz. trout fillets
salt to taste
pepper to taste
2 eggs, beaten
½ cup water
1 cup Italian seasoned bread crumbs
1 stick butter
Creole Sauce:
   1 stick butter
   1½ cups chopped green peppers

2⅓ cups chopped onions
½ cup chopped celery
2 16-oz. cans whole tomatoes plus juice
¼ cup dry white wine
6 bay leaves
1 tsp. sugar
1½ lbs. boiled crawfish tails or 1½ lbs.
   boiled peeled medium shrimp
1 tsp. salt
½ tsp. black pepper

To prepare the Creole sauce, melt 1 stick of butter in a frying pan. Sauté the green peppers, onions, and celery for 2–3 minutes. Add the tomatoes plus juice, wine, bay leaves, and sugar. Cover and simmer the sauce for 1 hour. Simmer the sauce uncovered for 45 minutes, stirring occasionally. Add the crawfish or shrimp, and cook the sauce for 10 minutes. Add the salt and pepper, and cook the sauce another minute.

To prepare the trout, salt and pepper each fillet. Dip the fillets in the eggs, which have been beaten with the water. Then dredge the fish in the bread crumbs.

In a large frying pan, sauté the fish in 1 stick of butter which has been melted to the bubbling point, and cook the fillets until they are flaky and golden brown.

Serve the fish hot with 1 cup Creole Sauce over each portion.

Serves 6.

Yellow Squash Marion

1 lb. fresh yellow squash	1 1/4 cups cracker meal
1 stick butter	1 tbs. sugar
1/2 cup chopped green onions with tops	1 tsp. thyme
1/4 lb. ground beef	1 tsp. salt
1/4 lb. lump crabmeat	1/4 tsp. pepper
2 cups milk	paprika
2 eggs, beaten	

Slice the squash, and boil it until it is tender (about 5–7 minutes). Drain the squash well, and mash it with a fork in a mixing bowl.

Melt the butter in a skillet, and sauté the green onions and ground beef until they are cooked (about 5–10 minutes). Stir the crabmeat in until well coated with the butter. Pour these sautéed ingredients into the bowl with the squash. Add the milk, 1 cup of cracker meal, and eggs, and mix well. Season the mixture with sugar, thyme, salt, and pepper.

Pour the mixture into a greased casserole, and top with 1/4 cup cracker meal and paprika. Bake the squash in a 350-degree oven for 30 minutes or until the top is browned and a knife inserted in the center comes out clean.

Serves 6.

Clockwise from top: Yellow Squash Marion, Banana Muffins, Oysters
Tchoupitoulas, Trout Creole, Bananas Tchoupitoulas.

Banana Muffins

4 tbs. (½ stick) butter or margarine	¾ cup mashed bananas
¾ cup sugar	1½ tsp. baking powder
1 egg, beaten	1¼ cups flour
1 tbs. vanilla extract	⅓ cup milk

In a mixing bowl, cream the butter or margarine and the sugar together. Add the egg
and vanilla extract. Blend in the mashed bananas. Add the dry ingredients and then
the milk. Grease the muffin tins, and fill them two-thirds full with the batter. Bake the
muffins at 375 degrees for 20–25 minutes, or until they are golden brown.

Yield: 12 muffins.

TUJAGUE'S
823 Decatur Street

The Guichet family has owned this historic restaurant for over seventy years, taking over from the side-by-side restaurants of Etienne Annouille and the legendary Madame Begue.

Philip Guichet was born in 1866 in Lafourche Parish, where his father Philibert owned the only rice mill on the Bayou in a small town called Guichetville, near Raceland. The family moved to New Orleans, and Philibert went into the restaurant business with Monsieur Tujague. When Tujague died, after having operated the restaurant since 1856, Philip and his friend John Castet bought the restaurant, making a pact that whoever survived would buy full ownership on the death of his partner. Castet died, and Guichet bought the restaurant. Philip's two sons, Philip and Otis, grew up in the business and took over full management on Philip Sr.'s retirement. Their duties were divided: Otis ran the dining room, and Philip Jr. ran the bar.

Philip Jr. became a celebrated mixologist and in 1928 won the New York contest for cocktail mixing. The contest was presided over by Walter Winchell, who agreed that the best entry was Philip's creation, the Grasshopper. The restaurant is currently managed by Philip and by Otis's son, Ronald.

Tujague's menu has not changed much over the years: it offers a table d'hôte eight-course dinner. The food is simple—boiled brisket, soups, gumbo. Nostalgia is a meal at Tujague's.

Shrimp Rémoulade

1 gallon water
1 package crab boil
3 tbs. salt
36 large shrimp
Rémoulade Sauce:
    1 cup ketchup

2 tbs. horseradish
2 tbs. yellow mustard
2 tsp. Worcestershire sauce
dash Tabasco
4 hard-boiled eggs, chopped
2 raw eggs, beaten

To make the rémoulade sauce, mix the ketchup, horseradish, mustard, Worcestershire sauce, Tabasco, hard-boiled eggs, and raw eggs in a bowl until well blended. Chill the sauce before serving.

In a large pot, bring the water, crab boil, and salt to a full boil. Add the shrimp. When the water returns to a boil, turn off the heat and allow the shrimp to sit in the pot for 5 minutes to absorb the seasonings. Drain the shrimp, let them cool, and peel them before serving.

Allow 4 tablespoons of rémoulade sauce and 6 shrimp per serving.

Serves 6.

Chicken Gumbo

1 3-lb. fryer, cut up (reserve giblets)
10–12 cups water
2 cups chopped yellow onions
2 tsp. salt
½ tsp. pepper
1 cup flour
½ cup vegetable oil

1½ cups chopped green onions
    (white and green parts)
1 cup finely chopped celery
½ lb. ham, diced
½ lb. andouille sausage, sliced
1 tbs. filé powder
cooked rice

In a large soup pot, boil the chicken giblets (but not the liver) in the water with the onions, salt, and pepper. Meanwhile, coat the chicken pieces with the flour, reserving 4 tablespoons of the flour for the roux. Add the oil to a large skillet, and fry the chicken pieces until they are browned but not completely cooked. Put the chicken in the soup pot with the giblets and onions, and simmer.

Drain off all but 4 tablespoons of oil from the skillet, and stir in the reserved 4 tablespoons of flour. Stirring constantly, cook the roux over low heat until it is medium-dark brown. Add the green onions and celery, and cook the mixture for 5 minutes more. Add this to the soup pot.

In the same frying pan, brown the ham and andouille over medium heat. Add this to the soup pot, and continue to simmer the gumbo for 30 minutes more. Turn off heat and stir in the filé powder until it is well blended. Do not allow the gumbo to boil after adding the filé powder. Taste the gumbo for seasoning.

Serve the gumbo over cooked rice.

Serves 6.

Brenda Gooden removing fresh pecan pies from oven.
Seafood gumbo and chicken gumbo are on the stove.

Boiled Beef

6 lbs. choice brisket of beef
10 cups cold water
2 onions, quartered
1½ ribs celery, quartered
1 head garlic, peeled (cloves may be
    crushed or left whole)
1 bay leaf

1 heaping tbs. salt
15 black peppercorns
Tujague's Boiled Beef Sauce:
    1 cup ketchup
    ½ cup Creole mustard
    ½ cup horseradish

Place the brisket in a large soup pot, and pour in the cold water. Add the onions, celery, garlic, bay leaf, salt, and peppercorns, and bring to a boil. Simmer for approximately 2¼ hours or until the beef is cooked and tender. Remove the beef from the stock, and slice it. Strain the stock, skim off the fat, and reserve it for other recipes.

Clockwise: Chicken Gumbo, Shrimp Rémoulade, Boiled Beef with Sauce, Pecan Pie.

Make Tujague's Boiled-Beef Sauce by combining the ketchup, mustard, and horse-radish until they are well blended.

Cut the boiled-beef into six pieces and serve each portion with ⅓ cup of the sauce for dipping.

Serves 6.

Pecan Pie

Pie Crust:
    1 cup all-purpose flour
    1 tsp. sugar
    ½ tsp. salt
    ⅓ cup shortening
    1 tbs. chilled butter
    2 tbs. cold water
3 eggs
1 cup sugar

⅔ cup dark Karo syrup
2 tbs. butter, melted
1 tsp. vanilla
⅛ tsp. salt
3 tbs. bourbon (or brandy, praline liqueur, or amaretto)
1½ cups pecan halves

Preheat the oven to 400 degrees.

In a bowl, mix together the flour, 1 teaspoon of sugar, and ½ teaspoon of salt. Blend in the shortening and 1 tablespoon of butter with a pastry cutter until they are thoroughly combined. The mixture should be crumbly. Pour in the cold water, and blend well to bind the dough. Shape the dough into a ball, place it on a flat, lightly floured surface, and roll it out with a lightly floured rolling pin. The dough should extend 2 inches beyond the 9-inch pie pan. Fit the dough in the pie pan, and crimp the edges.

In a mixing bowl, beat the eggs, and blend in 1 cup of sugar, the Karo syrup, 2 tablespoons of melted butter, the vanilla, and ⅛ teaspoon of salt. Stir in the bourbon and pecan halves.

Pour the mixture into the pie crust, and bake the pie in the oven for 10 minutes. Lower the heat to 350 degrees, and continue baking for about 30 minutes more or until the filling is set and the crust is browned.

Cool the pie on a wire rack before serving.

Serves 6–8.

THE VERSAILLES RESTAURANT

2100 St. Charles Avenue

The Versailles Restaurant is owned and operated by Gunter Preuss and his wife Evelyn. Both native Germans, they decided to visit the United States in 1960 and have remained here.

Gunter first learned his trade from his father, also a restaurateur. He worked and studied in hotels and restaurants in France, England, and Sweden.

Upon coming to America, Gunter spent four years in Kansas City, then moved to New York City, where he worked at the Statler Hilton. He soon became the youngest executive chef in the Hilton Hotel chain.

Washington was Gunter's next stop, where he assisted in opening the Hilton there. While he was there, he catered to such personages as Robert Kennedy, Lyndon Johnson, and Ronald Reagan.

The Preusses then moved to Chicago and San Francisco. They finally wound up at New Orleans. Gunter worked at the Fairmont for several years before opening the Versailles,

Gunter Pruess has worked hard and has proved himself and the Versailles in a city where the competition is tough and the restaurants are great.

Cream of Leek Chantilly

4 medium-size leeks, both white and green parts washed, each part finely chopped separately	5 tbs. flour
	2 chicken bouillon cubes
	2 bay leaves
13 cups water	1 cup heavy cream
1 tbs. minced garlic	¾ tsp. salt
4 tbs. butter	½ tsp. white pepper

Boil the green leek trimmings in the water for 30 minutes. Strain the stock, and reserve 6 cups.

Gently sauté the white part of the leeks and the garlic in the butter for 2–3 minutes or until they become translucent. Add the flour, and, stirring constantly, cook the mixture for 10 minutes. Do not brown the flour. Add the 6 cups of leek stock in three stages, mixing thoroughly after each addition. Add the bouillon cubes and bay leaves, and simmer gently for 25 minutes, stirring occasionally. Finally, add ½ cup of heavy cream, and season the soup with salt and pepper, adjusting the seasonings to your taste. Simmer the soup for 10 minutes more.

Meanwhile, whip the remaining ½ cup of heavy cream.

When the soup is done, serve each portion garnished with a dollop of whipped cream.

Serves 6.

Clockwise from top: Cream of Leek Chantilly, Veal Farci Versailles, Lemon Tequila Soufflé, Bouillabaisse, Crawfish Versailles.

Bouillabaisse

2 medium carrots, sliced thin
1 medium onion, chopped
3 ribs celery, chopped medium-fine
1 leek (white part only), sliced
1 fennel root (if available), chopped, or
 ½ tsp. fennel seeds
4 tbs. butter
1 tbs. tomato paste
½ cup brandy
1 cup white wine
1½ cups peeled, seeded, and diced
 tomatoes
½ tsp. finely chopped garlic
pinch of saffron, presoaked
6 cups fish broth (use shrimp shells and
 heads and the bones and skin from the
 fish fillet, below, plus 6 cups water)

1 lb. raw shrimp, peeled (reserve the
 shells and heads)
½ lb. skinless, boneless fish fillet, cut into
 1-inch pieces (reserve the bones and
 skin)
1 doz. freshly shucked oysters
3 medium-sized lobster tails, meat
 removed (about 1 lb.)
½ dozen mussels in shells, if available
2 tsp. salt or to taste
1 tsp. white pepper
1 cup fresh lump crabmeat
3–4 tbs. chopped parsley
garlic croutons, for garnish

In a soup pot, sauté the carrots, onion, celery, leek, and fennel in 2 tablespoons of butter for 3–4 minutes over medium-high heat. Add the tomato paste, and blend well. Flame with the brandy. Extinguish the flame with the wine. Add the tomatoes, garlic, and saffron. Add the fish broth, and cook the soup over medium heat for about 20 minutes or until the vegetables are done.

Separately sauté the shrimp, fish, oysters, lobster meat, and mussels in 2 tablespoons of butter for 2–3 minutes. Add the sautéed seafood to the soup pot, and cook the bouillabaisse for 10 minutes over medium heat. Add the salt and pepper and additional white wine to taste.

Serve the bouillabaisse topped with crabmeat and chopped parsley. Garnish each serving with garlic croutons.

Serves 6–8.

Veal Farci Versailles

Béchamel Sauce:
    1/2 stick butter
    4 tbs. flour
    1 1/2 cups milk, or 1 cup milk plus 1/2 cup
       fish stock
    1/2 cup heavy cream
    1 tsp. salt or to taste
    pinch white pepper
Demiglace:
    3 tbs. butter
    1/2 cup finely chopped onion
    1/2 cup finely chopped carrot
    3 tbs. flour
    3 cups beef or chicken stock
    1 tbs. tomato paste
    2 cloves garlic, minced
    1/2 tsp. dried thyme
    1 small rib celery, chopped
    2 bay leaves
    3 sprigs parsley
    salt to taste
    pepper to taste

Crawfish Versailles:
    2 tbs. sliced green onions
    1 tbs. minced shallots
    2 tbs. minced garlic
    2 tbs. butter
    1/2 cup white wine
    1 1/2 tsp. lemon juice
    1 1/2 tbs. fresh chopped dill or 1 tbs. dried
      dill
    1 1/2 lbs. fresh boiled crawfish tails
    1/2 tsp. salt or to taste
    1/8 tsp. cayenne
18 silver-dollar-sized medallions of milk-
    fed veal
salt to taste
pepper to taste
lemon juice
1 cup flour
4 eggs, beaten
1 stick of butter, clarified
chopped parsley

Prepare the béchamel by melting the butter in a small saucepan and stirring in the flour. Cook the roux over medium-low heat for 2–3 minutes. Remove the pan from the heat, and add the milk or the milk and stock. Stir the sauce, and bring it to the boiling point. Add the cream, salt, and pepper, and cook the béchamel for another 1/2 minute. Set the béchamel aside until you are ready to use it in the Crawfish Versailles recipe.

Prepare the demiglace by melting 2 tablespoons of the butter in a saucepan and adding the onion and carrot, cooking the vegetables until they begin to turn brown. Add the remaining tablespoon of butter, stir in the flour, and cook the roux until it is browned. Add the stock, tomato paste, garlic, thyme, celery, bay leaves, parsley, salt, and pepper. Bring the mixture to a boil, and simmer it for 30 minutes. Strain it.

To prepare the Crawfish Versailles, sauté the green onions, shallots, and garlic in the butter until the vegetables are tender, 2 minutes. Add the wine and lemon juice,

$\longrightarrow$

and reduce the liquid by one-half. Over medium heat this will take 3–4 minutes. Add the reserved béchamel and the dill, and cook 4–5 minutes more. Add the crawfish tails, and simmer the mixture for 10 minutes. Season the mixture with salt and cayenne.

Season the veal medallions with salt, pepper, and lemon juice. Dip them in the flour, shaking off any excess, and then dip them into the beaten eggs. Place the veal directly in a sauté pan with hot clarified butter. Sauté the medallions until they are golden.

To prepare each serving, place one medallion on a plate, and top the medallion with ½ cup heated Crawfish Versailles. Then put two more medallions over this, and spoon about 3 tablespoons demiglace over the top. Sprinkle the veal with fresh chopped parsley, and serve.

Serves 6.

Lemon Tequila Soufflé

⅔ cup sugar
1 cup water
6 egg yolks
⅓ cup white wine
5 tbs. lemon juice (Cut 6 large lemons in half. Squeeze the juice from them, strain the juice, and reserve the 5 tbs.

of juice for this recipe. Scoop out the pulp from the lemon halves and discard it, and freeze the lemon shells.)
3 tbs. tequila
1 cup heavy cream, ice cold
1 tbs. sugar
mint leaves, for garnish

Combine ⅔ cup sugar with the water in a saucepan, and boil the mixture gently until it begins to thicken. This will take approximately 15 minutes over medium heat. Remove the syrup from the heat, and let it cool thoroughly.

When the mixture is cool, add the egg yolks, wine. lemon juice, and tequila. Cook this mixture over low heat, whisking constantly, until it is slightly thickened and the foam recedes, approximately 10–12 minutes. Be sure that the eggs taste cooked. Place this mixture into the refrigerator to cool. Stir it occasionally.

Beat the heavy cream to the soft-peak stage, add 1 tablespoon of sugar, and continue beating until stiff peaks form. Fold ¾ cup of the whipped cream (reserving the rest for topping) into the cool lemon-tequila mixture. Place the mixture in the freezer for 2–3 hours before serving.

To serve, scoop the soufflé into the frozen lemon halves, and put the lemon halves in individual dessert glasses on a bed of shaved ice. The desserts can be frozen until ready to serve, or they may be served immediately with a garnish of whipped cream and a mint leaf.

Serves 6–12, depending on the size of the serving.

Orange Soufflé.

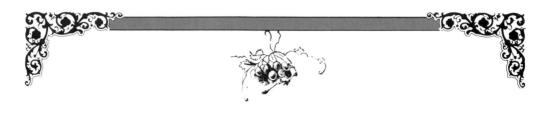

VISKO'S

516 Gretna Boulevard
Gretna, Louisiana

Visko's Restaurant is a popular West Bank eating establishment. Begun in 1970 by Vincent and Joe Voskovich and their mother, Visko's was a small take-out sandwich shop specializing in oyster poorboys. The shop gained popularity, the menu expanded, and the small shop grew into a restaurant.

Vincent and Joe's grandfather was a Yugoslavian who came to Louisiana and made his living as an oyster fisherman. His name was Visko, Yugoslavian for Vincent. Their father Matthew was also an oyster fisherman. Vincent and Joe had practically grown up on fishing boats and knew a great deal about seafood.

Dining rooms were added to the restaurant as it continued to grow until 1974, when it burned to the ground. Undaunted, the Voskovich family rebuilt an even larger and more well-appointed Visko's. Sister Faye began to help with the operation, and she and her brothers opened Visko's Steamroom next door. Vincent died several years ago, and the restaurants are now run by Faye and Joe. Visko's is still growing. A new dining room and new banquet rooms have just been added, and there is a need for more space.

Calamari Italia

2½ lbs. cleaned squid
1 lb. (4 sticks) butter
¼ cup finely chopped garlic

1 tsp. salt
¼ cup chopped parsley

To prepare the squid, cut off the tentacles about ½ inch below the eyes. Reserve the tentacles for this dish. Grasp the squid's head in one hand and the body in the other, and gently pull to remove the head and attached entrails from the body. Discard the head. Remove the spine (the delicate, transparent, feather-shaped part), and discard it. Holding the body up by the "tail," milk out any remaining entrails. Peel the spotted outer layer of skin from the body and fins. This will peel off easily. Slice the squid into 1/2-inch pieces, checking to make sure that they are clean of entrails. Rinse these pieces and the tentacles in a colander, and set them aside to drain thoroughly.

In a large skillet, heat the butter to bubbling. Add the garlic, and cook it, stirring, for 2 minutes. Mix in the squid, and simmer the squid for 10 minutes, stirring occasionally. Remove the skillet from the heat, and stir in the salt and chopped parsley.

Serve 4 ounces of calamari per person. Pour the hot garlic butter over the squid, and serve it with French bread for dipping.

Serves 6.

Shrimp and Crabmeat Salad

Shrimp and Crabmeat Dressing:
   1/2 cup prepared bleu-cheese dressing
     (available in groceries)
   1/2 cup mayonnaise
1 head iceberg lettuce

1/2 lb. boiled, peeled shrimp
1/2 lb. lump crabmeat
salt to taste
freshly ground black pepper to taste
12 cherry tomatoes for garnish

Make the dressing by blending the ingredients together until they are smooth. Set the dressing aside.

Wash the lettuce, and reserve 6 outer leaves to line the salad bowls. Shred or slice remainder of the lettuce.

Coarsely chop the shrimp, and mix the shrimp with the crabmeat. Combine the seafood mixture with an equal amount (approximately 3 cups) of shredded lettuce. Mix in 1/2 cup to 1 cup of the dressing. Season the mixture with salt and pepper.

Line six salad bowls with the 6 reserved lettuce leaves, and fill each leaf with 1/2 cup of salad. Garnish the salad with cherry tomatoes, and serve.

Serves 6.

Clockwise from top: Ice Cream with Praline Sauce, Calamari Italia, Oysters Meaux, Shrimp and Crabmeat Salad.

Oysters Meaux

Meaux Sauce:
    6 egg yolks
    2½ tbs. lemon juice
    ¼ tsp. white pepper
    ¼ tsp. cayenne
    2 sticks butter
    2 tbs. Meaux French mustard
3 doz. fresh oysters, shucked and drained
1 cup Visko's Fish Fry (or corn flour
    seasoned with Italian herbs, cayenne,
    and salt)

1 cup vegetable oil for frying
6 English muffins
1 tbs. melted butter
18 slices Canadian bacon
paprika for garnish
parsley sprigs for garnish
lime slices for garnish

To make the Meaux sauce, place the egg yolks, lemon juice, white pepper, and cayenne in a blender, and blend on medium speed for a few seconds.

218

In a saucepan, heat the butter to a bubbling boil, but do not brown it. With the blender on high speed, add the hot butter in a slow, steady stream until it is fully incorporated with the other ingredients. Add the mustard, and blend the sauce for a few more seconds on high speed.

Dredge the oysters in the fish fry, and fry them in the oil until they are golden brown. Set them aside, and keep them warm.

Split the English muffins in half, and place them open-faced in pairs on a cookie sheet. Brush the cut sides with the melted butter. Lay 3 slices of Canadian bacon on each open muffin—1 slice on each half and 1 slice overlapping the other two slices. Place the cookie sheet under the broiler until the bacon is thoroughly heated and the muffins are lightly toasted.

Top each serving of 2 muffin halves with 6 oysters. Pour 2 ounces (4 tablespoons) of Meaux sauce over each serving, and garnish with a sprinkling of paprika, a parsley sprig, and a slice of lime.

Serves 6.

Ice Cream with Praline Sauce

1 stick butter	2 tbs. dark rum
1 cup dark brown sugar	1 tsp. maple extract
¼ cup dark Karo syrup	1 cup chopped pecans
½ cup water	16 scoops vanilla ice cream

Melt the butter in a saucepan. Stir in the brown sugar. Add the Karo syrup and water, and cook the mixture over medium heat until it reaches the boiling point. Continue boiling the mixture for 1 minute, stirring constantly. Remove the pan from the heat, and allow the mixture to cool slightly. Stir in the rum, maple extract, and chopped pecans. The praline sauce will thicken as it cools.

Serve ¼ cup of praline sauce over 2 scoops of vanilla ice cream.

Store the sauce covered in the refrigerator.

Serves 8.

WILLY COLN'S RESTAURANT

2505 Whitney Avenue
Gretna, Louisiana

Willy Coln was born in Cologne, Germany. He and his wife Erna came to the United States in 1964. After working as a chef at the Royal Orleans Hotel, he was appointed executive chef of the Royal Sonesta Hotel in 1972.

Willy and Erna opened their own restaurant in 1976. Located obscurely on Whitney Avenue in Gretna, Louisiana, Willy believed that if the restaurant were excellent, people would come. And come they did. Willy and Erna have worked very hard to build the restaurant into what is now considered one of New Orleans' best.

The Colns have expanded, renovated, and redecorated the building. The result of their labors is New Orleans–Bavarian with a touch of the Caribe.

Seviche

½ lbs. fresh redfish or any firm fish, cut into ¼–½-inch dice

½ lb. fresh shrimp, cut into ¼–½-inch dice

½ lb. fresh scallops, cut into ¼–½-inch dice

½ cup fresh lime juice

½ cup lemon juice

2 cups diced onion (approximately 1 large onion)

2 cups peeled, seeded, and diced tomatoes (approximately 3 medium tomatoes)

1 cup diced bell pepper (approximately 1 large pepper)

½ tsp. minced garlic

1 red hot pepper, minced, or ¼ tsp. cayenne

1 tsp. dried thyme leaves

1 tsp. Worcestershire sauce

1/16 tsp. powdered cloves

1 tsp. salt

½ cup olive oil

Place all the ingredients in a shallow dish, and marinate the fish, shrimp and scallops for 2 hours, turning them frequently. Serve cold.

Serves 6–8.

Bahamian Chowder

4 oz. peeled and deveined raw shrimp

4 oz. fresh fish, diced

1 tbs. finely chopped parsley leaves
and stems

1 medium carrot, julienned

1 small bell pepper, julienned

2 green onions, julienned

1 medium onion, julienned

1 stalk celery, julienned

2 medium tomatoes, julienned

2 tbs. olive oil

2 tbs. flour

1 large bay leaf

1 medium garlic clove, minced

2 tbs. tomato paste

½ cup dry white wine

1½ quarts fish stock

½ tsp. dried thyme leaves

⅛ tsp. cayenne

¼ tsp. black pepper

¼ tsp. salt

Sauté the fish, shrimp, and vegetables in the hot oil for 2 minutes. Dust the mixture with the flour. Stir the mixture until the flour is blended. Add the bay leaf, garlic, tomato paste, white wine, and fish stock to the mixture. Add the seasonings to taste. Bring the chowder to a boil, and simmer it for 5 minutes.

Serves 6–8.

Ingredients for Seviche.

Roast Veal Shank

2 3½-lb, milk-fed veal shanks
salt
pepper
1 cup diced celery
1 cup diced carrots
1 cup diced onions
2 cups beef or meat stock or bouillon
1 cup packed julienned carrots (about 2
 medium carrots)

1 cup packed julienned zucchini (about 1
 medium zucchini)
1 cup packed julienned onion (about 1
 medium onion)
1 cup packed julienned cauliflower florets
24 small whole mushrooms
½ stick butter
salt to taste
black pepper to taste

Rub the veal shanks thoroughly with salt and pepper. Place the shanks in a roasting pan, and place the pan in a 450-degree oven. Roast the shanks uncovered for ½ hour. Add the diced celery, carrots, and onions to the pan, and pour in 1 cup of the stock. Cover the pan, and cook the shanks at 300 degrees for another ½ hour. Remove the pan from the oven. Add the second cup of stock, and baste the shanks with the pan juices. Return the shanks, uncovered, to the oven, and cook them for approximately 1½ hours, basting every ½ hour.

Remove the shanks from pan. Strain the juices and vegetables from roasting pan, reserving the juices and discarding the vegetables. Remove the fat as it rises to the top of the strained juices.

In a large frying pan, stir-fry or pan-sauté the julienned carrots, zucchini, onion, cauliflower, and the mushrooms in the butter for 4–5 minutes over medium high heat. The vegetables should be served al dente or crispy. Add salt and pepper to taste, and serve the vegetables over the warmed veal shanks. Serve the juice on the side.

Serves 6.

Clockwise from top right: Black Forest Cake, Roast Veal Shank, Bahamian Chowder, Lavosh (in background), Seviche.

Lavosh

1 package (¼ oz.) active dry yeast
1½ tsp. sugar
1 cup plus 2 tbs. warm water (110–115
  degrees)

3 cups all-purpose flour
½ stick butter, melted
1 tbs. white sesame seeds, chopped
  onions, or poppy seeds

Pour the yeast into a clean, small shallow bowl. Add 1 teaspoon of the sugar and ¼ cup of the warm water to the bowl. Let the mixture stand for 2–3 minutes, then stir the mixture to dissolve the yeast completely. Place the bowl in a warm, draft-free place for 5–10 minutes or until the mixture looks foamy and has almost doubled in volume.

Measure the flour into a mixing bowl, and make a well in the center of the flour. Pour in the yeast mixture, the remaining water and sugar, and the melted butter. Mix the ingredients well with a spoon until a soft, spongy dough is formed. Cover the bowl loosely with a warm, damp cloth, and return it to the warm, draft-free spot until the dough again doubles in volume, about 45 minutes.

Preheat the oven to 350 degrees.

When the dough has risen, place it on a lightly floured surface, and divide it into six equal parts. With a lightly floured rolling pin, roll each part into a flat round about ¼-inch thick. Place 2 or 3 rounds on each of two or three cookie sheets. Rub the surface of the rounds lightly with cool water, and sprinkle each one with ½ teaspoon sesame seeds or other topping.

Bake the rounds in the oven on the bottom rack for about 20 minutes or until the breads are a pale golden brown. (Bake the breads in "shifts" if oven size does not allow the entire recipe to be baked at once.) With a spatula transfer the breads to wire racks to cool. The breads will keep several days if stored in a dry, air-tight place.

Yield: 6 breads.

WINSTON'S PLACE

Hilton Hotel
2 Poydras Street

In 1976, when the Hilton Hotel was constructed, plans for Winston's Place were formulated for the plaza in front of the hotel. The Hilton management wanted an outstanding dining room in a food-conscious city.

At present the prix-fixe menu, which is delivered orally by Winston's service people, offers three or four choices per course. The idea is to use as many fresh items as possible, to take advantage of seasonal produce. In this way the chef is able to be creative and can buy the products he wants most to work with.

As a testament to the innovativeness of Winston's Place, alligator in season, white truffles, black morels, and Adriatic scampi are some of the items which will soon be introduced in a once-a-month specialty meal.

Stuffed Shrimp Calypso

Avocado Purée:
    1 ripe avocado
    1/3 cup oil
    4 tbs. lemon juice
    1/2 tsp. finely chopped garlic
    1/2 tsp. salt
    1/8 tsp. black pepper
Stuffing:
    1/2 lb. lump crabmeat
    3 tbs. homemade or prepared mayonnaise
    2 tbs. ketchup

1 tbs. brandy
1/2 tsp. dried tarragon leaves
1/4 tsp. salt
1/8 tsp. black pepper
1/8 tsp. Tabasco
water
salt
pepper
juice from 1/2 lemon
18 jumbo-size shrimp, uncooked

Scoop out the insides of the avocado, and combine it with the rest of the purée ingredients in a blender or food processor. Blend the purée for 2–3 minutes until it is thick. Chill the purée until you are ready to assemble the dish.

→

To make the stuffing, lightly fold together all of the stuffing ingredients. Chill the stuffing until you are ready to assemble the dish.

Season a pot of water with salt, pepper, and lemon juice, and bring it to a boil. Meanwhile, skewer the underbelly of each shrimp lengthwise with a toothpick. This is to prevent the shrimp from curling. Drop the shrimp into the boiling water, and bring the water back to a boil. Cook the shrimp 1 minute, drain, and let them cool.

To butterfly the shrimp, remove almost all of the shell, leaving the tail intact. Make a lengthwise incision on the underbelly of each shrimp, cutting almost through the shrimp. Splay open the shrimp, and devein it.

To serve, place 3 tablespoons of purée on each plate. Fill each shrimp with 1 tablespoon of the crabmeat stuffing. Place 3 stuffed shrimp over the purée on each plate, and serve.

Serves 6.

Oysters Churchill

Béarnaise Sauce:
    1 tsp. finely chopped French shallots or
      green onions
    2 tbs. tarragon vinegar
    3 tbs. dry white wine
    1 tsp. coarsely ground black pepper
    3 tbs. cold water
    4 egg yolks
    1/2 tsp. salt
    1 tbs. lemon juice
    1 1/2 sticks butter, melted and cooled to
      room temperature
    1 tsp. dried tarragon leaves
    1/2 tsp. finely chopped parsley
Mushroom Mixture:
    1 tbs. butter

    8 oz. mushrooms, finely chopped
    1 1/2 tbs. chopped French shallots or green
      onions (white and green parts)
    1/4 cup dry white wine
    1/4 tsp. salt
    1/8 tsp. black pepper
2 9-inch by 12-inch sheets of puff pastry,
    1/8–1/4 inch thick (see Note)
9–10 oz. goose-liver pâté, cut into 24
    bite-size pieces
24 small oysters or oyster pieces, well
    drained
1 egg, beaten

Prepare the Béarnaise sauce before the assembly of the other ingredients. Over low heat, boil the shallots, vinegar, white wine, and pepper until the mixture is almost dry. Transfer these ingredients into the top of a double boiler, and add the cold water, egg yolks, salt, and lemon juice. Over barely simmering water whisk the mixture until the mixture appears thick and glossy. Remove the sauce from the heat. Add the melted, cooled butter in a slow stream, whisking constantly until it is incorporated in the sauce. Strain the sauce. Add the tarragon leaves and parsley. Reheat the sauce slowly just before serving.

Prepare the mushroom mixture by melting the butter in a skillet and sautéeing the mushrooms and shallots. Add the white wine, and simmer the mixture until the liquid is reduced. Remove the mixture from the heat and set it aside until you are ready to use it.

Cut each 9 by 12-inch rectangle of puff pastry into twelve 3-inch squares. The dough will be easier to work with if it is very cold. In the middle of each square place 1 heaping teaspoon of the cooled mushroom mixture. Top this with a piece of pâté, and place an oyster on top of that. Fold over the puff pastry to form a triangle, and seal the edges of the pastry with your fingertips. The edges can be lightly moistened with water to form a tight seal.

Place the triangles on a greased cookie sheet, and brush them lightly with the beaten egg. Bake the pastries at 400 degrees for 20–25 minutes until they are crisped and browned. Serve them hot with the Béarnaise sauce.

Note: You may use Pepperidge Farm Puff Pastry. The pastries can be assembled ahead of time, refrigerated or frozen, and then brought to room temperature before baking.

Serves 6 as appetizer.

Fillet of Beef Waldorf

6 large artichokes
water
2 tbs. salt
1 large potato, peeled and cut into at least
   6 ½-inch slices
3 cups cold water
salt
pepper
vegetable oil for frying
Mushroom Sauce:
   ½ stick butter
   1 tbs. finely chopped French shallots or
     green onions

3 cups sliced mushrooms
1 tsp. flour
1 cup heavy cream
¼ tsp. salt
⅛ tsp. black pepper
1 egg yolk
6 8-oz. tenderloins
salt to taste
pepper to taste
melted butter

In a large pot boil the artichokes in water to cover to which has been added about 2 tablespoons salt. When the artichokes are tender, remove them from the water, and cool them. Remove the leaves from the artichokes, and expose the bottoms. Trim the bottoms so they will sit flat. Set the bottoms aside. Just before serving, warm the bottoms in hot water.

In a saucepan place the potato slices in approximately 3 cups of cold water, and bring to a boil. Continue boiling for 2–3 minutes. Drain the water from the potatoes, and pat the potatoes dry on a paper towel. Sprinkle both sides of the potato slices with salt and pepper, and fry the potatoes in vegetable oil until they are crisp and golden brown. Drain the potatoes, and keep them warm until they are ready to serve.

The sauce can be made in advance and reheated. To prepare the sauce, melt the butter in a saucepan, and sauté the shallots and mushrooms for about 10 minutes over medium heat until the water is cooked out of the mushrooms. Sprinkle the shallots and mushrooms with flour, and mix thoroughly. Add the heavy cream, and reduce it by half (cook over low heat for about 20 minutes). Add the salt and pepper. Just before serving, add the egg yolk to the warm sauce, and mix gently.

Prepare the tenderloin fillets by sprinkling them with salt and pepper. Baste them with butter, and broil them to your liking.

To serve, place a slice of fried potato on each plate, top the potato with a fillet, and crown each fillet with an artichoke bottom. Top this with approximately 3 tablespoons of the mushroom sauce. Serve the dish hot.

Serves 6.

Mongolian Rack of Lamb

6 racks of spring lamb or 3 2-lb. racks of lamb (have the butcher remove the chine bones)
Marinade:
    ½ cup soy sauce
    1 clove garlic, crushed
    1 tsp. finely chopped fresh ginger

black pepper
Glaze:
    ¼ cup apricot glaze (if unavailable, heat
       ½ cup apricot preserves and strain)
    ¼ cup soy sauce
    ½ tsp. finely chopped fresh ginger
    1 garlic clove, minced

To make the marinade, combine all the marinade ingredients.

Cut the excess fat off the lamb, and marinate the lamb racks overnight in the marinade mixture.

Bring the lamb to room temperature.

About 20 minutes before serving, sprinkle the lamb racks with black pepper, and baste them with the marinade.

Make the glaze by combining all the glaze ingredients.

Preheat oven to 400 degrees, and roast the spring lamb racks for 5–6 minutes on each side. If you are using 2-pound racks, cook them for 10 minutes on each side. Brush the rounded side of the racks with the apricot glaze, and roast the small racks 2–3 minutes more and the larger racks 5 minutes more.

Slice the lamb racks, and serve them with the pan juices on the side. Steamed rice makes a good accompaniment.

Serves 6.

Clockwise from top: Breast of Duck in Mourning, Fried Camembert with Lingenberry Sauce, Medallions of Veal Cortez, Turbines of Sole, Mongolian Rack of Lamb, House Salad, Tournedos Madagascar, Oysters Churchill (in center).

Poached Pears with Coriander Sauce and
Cornets Stuffed with Ginger Cream

Poaching Liquid:
    4 cups sugar
    2 bottles Bordeaux
    1 cinnamon stick
    3 whole cloves
    1 orange, halved
    2 lemons, halved
    1 tbs. anise seeds or fennel seeds
6 pears, peeled and cored from the
  bottom, leaving the stem intact
Coriander Sauce:
    2 cups milk
    $1/2$ cup sugar
    1 inch vanilla bean
    1 tbs. crushed coriander seeds
    6 egg yolks, well beaten and brought to
      room temperature

$1/4$ bunch of coriander leaves, finely
    chopped. (If unavailable, use 2 tbs.
    finely chopped parsley mixed with 2 tbs.
    finely chopped fresh basil.)
Ginger Cream:
    1 stick butter, room temperature
    $1/2$ cup sugar
    $3^1/2$ tbs. fresh gingerroot, peeled and
      grated
    1 egg, room temperature
    $1/4$ cup flour
Cornets:
    $1/2$ cup flour
    $1/2$ cup plus 2 tbs. powdered sugar
    $1/2$ stick unsalted butter, room temperature
    2 egg whites
    1 egg yolk

Combine all the ingredients for the poaching liquid. Poach the pears in the liquid by simmering them for 12 minutes. Remove the pears from the heat, let them cool, and refrigerate them overnight in the poaching liquid. Remove the pears from the liquid to serve.

Make the coriander sauce. Bring the milk, sugar, vanilla, and coriander seeds to a boil. Strain the mixture. Add a small portion of the strained milk mixture to the beaten egg yolks. Then pour the egg yolks back into the milk, and place the mixture in the top of a double boiler. Cook the mixture until the sauce reaches a thick, creamy consistency. Add the coriander leaves. Chill the sauce.

To make the ginger cream, cream the butter and sugar together. Add the ginger, and mix. Add the egg, and beat well. Finish by sifting the flour over the mixture. Mix well. Refrigerate the ginger cream before piping it into the cornets.

To make the cornets, mix the flour and sugar together. Cream the butter, and whip in the flour and sugar. Add the unbeaten egg whites one by one. Whip well after

→

each addition. Add the egg yolk, and beat again. Let the batter stand for several hours.

Preheat the oven to 400 degrees.

Drop the cookie mixture onto a well-greased cookie sheet by the level tablespoonful. Leave at least 2 inches of space between the cookies for them to spread. Bake the cookies in the oven until the edges are brown but the center is still pale. Remove the cookies from the oven, and, while they are still hot and pliable, remove them from the cookie sheet and wrap them around a cone-shaped mold. Remove the mold, and the cookie will hold the cone shape as it cools. You will need to work fast since the cookies will begin to harden on the cookie sheet. You may want to bake only a few at a time to avoid this.

When all the cornets are cooled, pipe the ginger cream into them with a pastry bag.

To serve, put 1 pear on each of six plates. Pour about $\frac{1}{4}$ cup of cold coriander sauce over each serving. Garnish each plate with 2 ginger-cream-stuffed cornets.

Serves 6.

INDEX